'A great book on a not-so-easy subject!'
– MICHAEL D. COE, author of *Breaking the* _____

T0024713

'*The Indus* is very well written and eminently readable . . .
Andrew Robinson deals with all the unsolved problems in
a fair manner and with balanced judgement . . . a valuable
contribution to the literature on the Indus civilization.'
– IRAVATHAM MAHADEVAN, author of *The Indus Script:
Texts, Concordance and Tables*

'A very well-written, well-illustrated popular account of the
Indus civilization . . . This new work is an important addition
to the literature because of the author's extensive knowledge of
the subject, his use of the most recent sources, and his succinct
but engaging style.' – *Choice*

'Cleverly weaves a rich and intricate tapestry of life in the
third millennium BC . . . All aspects of the discourse on
the Indus world, whether secular-mundane or religious-
sacred, are subjected to Robinson's penetrative analysis
and intellectual rigour.' – *Dawn*

'Robinson writes with an elegant clarity which comes from
a masterly overview of the subject and transmits some of the
mysterious excitement which this enigmatic civilisation evokes.'
– *Journal of the Royal Asiatic Society*

'Andrew Robinson's new book is a clear summary of what we
know, and a tantalising account of what we might yet know . . .
Robinson does a commendable job of laying out the evidence
in all its incompleteness and ambiguity.' – *Minerva*

LOST CIVILIZATIONS

The books in this series explore the rise and fall of the great civilizations and peoples of the ancient world. Each book considers not only their history but their art, culture and lasting legacy and asks why they remain important and relevant in our world today.

Already published:

The Aztecs Frances F. Berdan
The Barbarians Peter Bogucki
Egypt Christina Riggs
The Etruscans Lucy Shipley
The Goths David M. Gwynn
The Greeks Philip Matyszak
The Indus Andrew Robinson
The Persians Geoffrey Parker and Brenda Parker
The Sumerians Paul Collins

THE
INDUS
LOST CIVILIZATIONS

ANDREW ROBINSON

REAKTION BOOKS

For Asko Parpola
Scholar, decipherer and friend

Published by Reaktion Books Ltd
Unit 32, Waterside
44–48 Wharf Road
London N1 7UX, UK

www.reaktionbooks.co.uk

First published 2015, reprinted 2016
First paperback edition published 2021
Copyright © Andrew Robinson 2015

Printed and bound in Great Britain
by Bell & Bain, Glasgow

A catalogue record for this book is available from the British Library

ISBN 978 1 78914 385 0

CONTENTS

# CHRONOLOGY

c. 7000–2600 BC	Village habitation at Mehrgarh (Baluchistan): wheat and barley cultivation, domestication of cattle
c. 5000 BC	Rice cultivation in China and India (Ganges valley)
Middle of 4th millennium BC	Urbanization at Uruk, Mesopotamia
c. 3500 BC	Settlement at Harappa (Punjab)
c. 3500–2600 BC	Early period of Indus civilization
c. 3100 BC	Cuneiform script begins in Mesopotamia; hieroglyphic script begins in Egypt
First half of 3rd millennium BC	Gilgamesh of Uruk reigns, Mesopotamia
c. 2600–2500 BC	Pyramids constructed at Giza, Egypt
c. 2600 BC	First Dynasty of Ur, Mesopotamia: trade between Mesopotamia and Indus valley begins

c. 2600–1900 BC	Mature period of Indus civilization: cities at Harappa and Mohenjo-daro (Sindh); Indus script is used throughout the civilization
c. 2400–1500 BC	Bactria and Margiana Archaeological Complex (BMAC), Turkmenistan and Afghanistan
c. 2334–2279 BC	Sargon of Akkad reigns, Mesopotamia; trades with Meluhha (Indus valley)
2nd millennium BC	Indo-Aryan-speaking peoples migrate from west into northwest India
c. 1900–1700 BC	Late period of Indus civilization: cities and Indus script decline
c. 1900–1500 BC	Alphabet begins in Egypt, Palestine and Sinai
c. 1800 BC	Trade between Mesopotamia and Indus valley declines
1792–1750 BC	Hammurabi of Babylon reigns, Mesopotamia
c. 1600–1050[?] BC	Shang civilization, China: Chinese character script develops
c. 1500–500 BC	Composition of Rigveda, followed by other Vedic literature in Sanskrit
1361–1352 BC	Tutankhamun reigns, Egypt
c. 1300 BC	Harappa ceases to be inhabited

c. 1200 BC	Collapse of civilization in eastern Mediterranean (Knossos, Mycenae, Troy, New Kingdom Egypt and others)
c. 800 BC	Cities begin in Ganges valley
563–483[?] BC	Life of Siddhartha Gautama, founder of Buddhism
522–486 BC	Darius the Great reigns in Persia
326 BC	Alexander the Great invades Indus valley
c. 300 BC–AD 400	Composition of Hindu epics *Ramayana* and *Mahabharata*
c. 269–232 BC	Reign of Asoka; Brahmi and Kharosthi scripts begin
AD 1921–4	Indus civilization discovered; excavation begins
1947	Partition of Indus sites between Pakistan and India
1980	Mohenjo-daro inscribed in list of World Heritage Sites by UNESCO

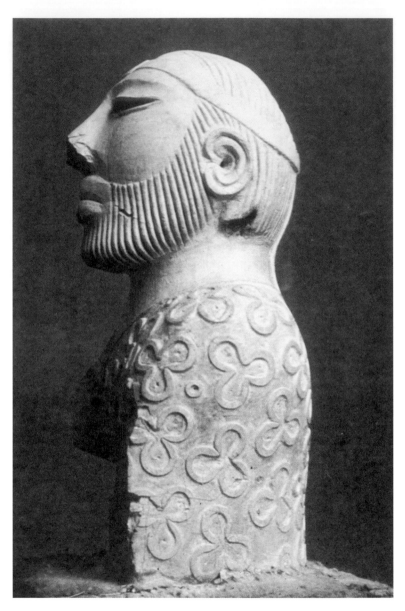

Bust of the 'priest-king', from Mohenjo-daro in the Indus valley.

ONE
AN ENIGMATIC
WORLD

In *Civilisation*, Kenneth Clark's study of Western civilization based on his pioneering 1960s television series, the eminent art historian pondered the non-Western origins of civilization two-and-a-half millennia before the classical Greeks. He observed:

> three or four times in history man has made a leap forward that would have been unthinkable under ordinary evolutionary conditions. One such time was about the year 3000 BC, when quite suddenly civilisation appeared, not only in Egypt and Mesopotamia but also in the Indus valley; another was in the sixth century BC, when there was not only the miracle of Ionia and Greece – philosophy, science, art, poetry, all reaching a point that wasn't reached again for two thousand years – but also in India a spiritual enlightenment that has perhaps never been equalled.[1]

Ancient Egypt and ancient Mesopotamia are familiar to the world, because of their art, architecture and royal burials; their extensive texts written in Egyptian hieroglyphs and Sumerian and Babylonian cuneiform; and numerous references to the Egyptian pharaohs and Babylonian and Persian rulers in the Hebrew Bible and Greek and Roman literature. So, too, are the glories of classical Greece and, maybe less so, the spirituality of Buddhist India (roughly contemporary with Greek philosophy) and early Hindu India as expressed in the Vedic literature (probably composed between 1500 and 500 BC). Not so familiar, however, is the civilization that appeared in the Indus valley – in what is now Pakistan and India – during the first half of the third millennium BC.

The Indus civilization was, in its own way, as extraordinary as the civilizations of Egypt and Mesopotamia. But it declined around the nineteenth century BC and left no direct legacy in the Indian subcontinent. Neither Alexander the Great, who invaded India from the northwest in the fourth century BC, nor Asoka Maurya, the great Buddhist-oriented emperor who ruled most of the subcontinent in the third century BC, was even dimly aware of the Indus civilization; nor were the Arab, Mughal and European colonial rulers of India during the next two millennia. Indeed, amazing as it may seem, the Indus civilization remained altogether invisible until the 1920s, when it was almost accidentally discovered at Harappa in the Punjab by British and Indian archaeologists (during Clark's youth). Ever since then, scholars have been trying to elucidate its mysteries, including the meanings encoded in the characters of its aesthetically exquisite but stubbornly undeciphered writing system, and thereby to elevate this most significant of 'lost' civilizations to the position it deserves – both in the history of South Asia and in world history.

Mohenjo-daro, one of two leading cities of the Indus civilization along with Harappa, seen from the air. It is located in southern Pakistan near the Indus river.

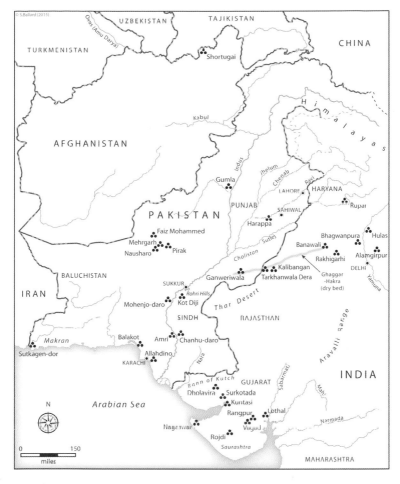

Map showing the most important of the approximately 1,000 sites of the Indus civilization and adjacent areas. Most sites belong to the Mature period, c. 2600–1900 BC, but some are older, in one case as early as 7000 BC.

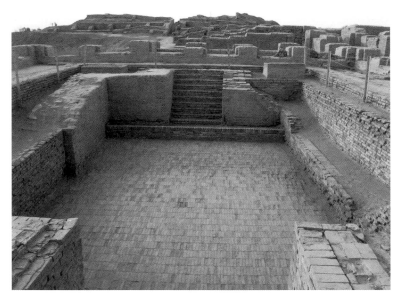

The Great Bath, Mohenjo-daro.

Archaeologists have identified well over a thousand settlements belonging to the Indus civilization in its various phases. They cover at least 800,000 square kilometres of what in 1947 became Pakistan and India – an area approximately a quarter the size of Western Europe – with an original population of perhaps one million people (the same as that of ancient Rome at its height). This was the most extensive urban culture of its time, about twice the size of its equivalent in Egypt or Mesopotamia. Though most Indus settlements were villages, some were towns, and at least five were substantial cities. The two largest cities, Mohenjo-daro and Harappa, located some 600 kilometres apart beside the Indus river and one of its many tributaries, were comparable with cities like Memphis in Egypt and Ur in Mesopotamia during the 'Mature' period of the Indus civilization, that is, between about 2600 and 1900 BC. Their maximum populations probably never exceeded 50,000, although life expectancy was good, judging from human bones in the cemetery at Harappa: nearly half of the individuals reached their mid-30s and almost one-sixth lived beyond the age of 55

However, the cities, despite their excellent brick-built construction, do not boast pyramids, palaces, temples, graves, statues, paintings or hoards of gold like those found in Egypt and Mesopotamia. Their grandest building is the so-called Great Bath at Mohenjo-daro, the earliest public water tank in the ancient world, a rectangle measuring 12 metres by 7 metres, with two wide staircases to the north and south leading down to a brick floor at a maximum depth of 2.4 metres, made watertight by a thick layer of bitumen. Though technically astonishing for its time, without doubt, the Great Bath was totally unadorned by carving or painting, so far as archaeologists can tell.

Yet Indus society, fed by crops watered by the great river and its many tributaries flowing from the Himalayas, was remarkably productive and sophisticated in other ways. For example, the Indus dwellers constructed ocean-going merchant ships that sailed as far as the Persian Gulf and the river-based cities of Mesopotamia, where Indus-made jewellery, weights, inscribed seals and other objects have been excavated, dating back to around 2500 BC. Mesopotamian cuneiform inscriptions refer to the Indus region by the name Meluhha, the precise meaning of which is unknown. The Indus cities' drainage and sanitation were two millennia ahead of those of the Roman empire; besides the Great Bath, they included magnificent circular wells, elaborate drains running beneath corbelled arches and the world's first toilets. The cities' well-planned streets, generally laid out in the cardinal directions, put to shame all but the town planning of the twentieth century AD. Some of their many personal ornaments, such as the necklaces of finely drilled, biconical carnelian beads up to 13 centimetres in length found in the royal cemetery of Ur in Mesopotamia, rival the treasures of the Egyptian pharaohs. Their binary/decimal system of standardized weights – consisting of stone cubes and truncated spheres – is unique in the ancient world, suggesting a highly developed economy. And the partially pictographic characters and vivid animal and human motifs of the tantalizing Indus script, inscribed on small seal stones and terracotta tablets, occasionally on metal, form 'little masterpieces of controlled realism, with a monumental strength in one sense out of all proportion to their size and in another entirely related to it', enthused the best-known excavator of the Indus civilization, Mortimer Wheeler.[2] Once seen, the seal stones are never forgotten – as witness the more than 100 differing decipherments of the Indus script proffered since the 1920s, some of them by distinguished academics such as the Egyptologist Flinders Petrie (not to mention many amateurs and cranks).

Indus archaeology has come a long way in almost a century. Nonetheless, it throws up many more unanswered fundamental

Indus seal stone showing a 'unicorn', a ritual offering stand and signs, made of steatite, from Mohenjo-daro. The writing system is yet to be deciphered.

questions than the archaeology of ancient Egypt and Mesopotamia (and China). A 'great cloud of unknowns . . . hangs over the civilisation', noted an Indus scholar, Jane McIntosh, in 2002.[3] Moreover, although excavation continues in both Pakistan and India, less than 10 per cent of the just over 1,000 Mature-period settlements have been excavated. Important clues, including further inscriptions, unquestionably remain to be dug up, as has happened in the past two or three decades. But, given the already extensive excavation of the cities, it does not seem likely that new discoveries will solve all of the current questions about the Indus civilization. Therefore this book, like all books on the subject, must mix hard information from archaeology with informed speculation in trying to answer these questions.

In particular, was the civilization an indigenous development, apparently emerging from neighbouring Baluchistan, where there is ample evidence for village settlement at Mehrgarh as early as 7000 BC? Or was it stimulated by the growth of civilization in not-so-distant Mesopotamia during the fourth millennium BC? What type of authority held together such an evidently organized, uniform and widespread society, if it truly did manage to prosper without palaces, royal graves, temples, powerful rulers and even priests? Why does the Indus civilization offer no definitive evidence for warfare, in the form of defensive fortifications, metal weapons and warriors – a situation without parallel in war-addicted ancient Mesopotamia, Egypt and China, not to mention all subsequent civilizations? Was the Indus religion the origin of Hinduism? Or is the apparent resemblance of some Indus seal iconography and practices to much later Hindu iconography and practices, such as the worship of the god Shiva and the caste system, based on wishful thinking? Is the Indus language that is written in the undeciphered script (assuming only a single written Indus language) related to still-existing Indian languages, such as the Dravidian languages of south India or the Sanskritic languages of north India? Lastly, why did the Indus civilization decline after about 1900 BC, and why did it leave no trace in the historical record? The characters of the Indus script seem to have become indecipherable almost four thousand years ago with the civilization's decline. They certainly bear no resemblance to the next writing that appeared in India, after an enormous gap of a millennium and a half: the Brahmi and Kharosthi alphabetic scripts used to write the rock and pillar inscriptions of the emperor Asoka in the third century BC, which were modelled on an alphabetic script from West Asia.

Scores of archaeologists and linguists – from Europe, India and Pakistan, Japan, Russia and the United States – have suggested answers to these fascinating questions. But inevitably they have been obliged to speculate; there can be no overall consensus, for lack of sufficient archaeological evidence and because the Indus script is mute.

To complicate matters, some of the debates have acquired a partisan political edge. The discovery of the Indus civilization understandably promoted national pride during India's movement towards independence from British rule in the 1930s and '40s. Its first excavator, John Marshall, started the trend in 1931 by claiming that 'the religion of the Indus peoples . . . is so characteristically Indian as hardly to be distinguishable from living Hinduism.'[4] The Indian nationalist leader Jawaharlal Nehru, before he became prime minister of independent India, noted, reasonably enough: 'It is surprising how much there is in Mohenjo-daro and Harappa which reminds one of persisting traditions and habits – popular ritual, craftsmanship, even some fashions in dress.'[5] Since then, however, and especially since the 1980s, Hindu nationalists in India have gone much further, disregarding archaeological and linguistic evidence in support of an openly political agenda. They are keen to recruit the Indus civilization as the *fons et origo* of Indian civilization, untainted by outside influence. According to them, it was the originator of the language of the Vedic literature, Sanskrit. This they view as an indigenous language, rather than as one descendant among many languages of a proto-Indo-European language that originated in the Pontic-Caspian steppes of southern Russia during the fourth millennium BC and reached India in the second millennium BC via Indo-Aryan-speaking migrants from Central Asia – the dominant view among non-Indian scholars regarding the origin of Sanskrit. They also view the Indus civilization as the originator of an early form of Hinduism. Thus, the Hindu nationalists promote the Indus civilization as the source of a continuous Indian identity dating back more than five millennia.

In the late 1990s certain Indian historians wishing to rewrite school textbooks at the behest of India's new Hindu nationalist government, appealed to a new book, *The Deciphered Indus Script*, written by two Indians with some linguistic and scientific credentials. Its authors, N. Jha and N. S. Rajaram, made astounding claims, announced to the Indian press in 1999 and published in 2000. The Indus script was said to be even older than had been thought (the mid-third millennium BC), dating back to the mid-fourth millennium BC, making it the world's oldest readable writing, pre-dating Mesopotamian cuneiform and Egyptian hieroglyphs. It apparently employed some kind of alphabet, two millennia older than the world's earliest-known alphabets from the Near East. Perhaps most sensational of all, at least for Indians, the Indus inscriptions were supposedly written in Vedic Sanskrit; one of them was found to mention a crucial Vedic river, the Saraswati, albeit obliquely ('Ila surrounds the blessed land').[6] This river, highly revered in the Rigveda, is today not visible above ground as a single stream, but is nevertheless known from ground surveys to have been a major river during the Indus civilization. Surveys on the Pakistani side of the India/Pakistan desert border region conducted in the 1970s and after have traced much, though not all, of the Saraswati's former course, part of which flowed in parallel with the Indus rather than as its tributary. In the course of their surveying, archaeologists (led by Mohammed Rafique Mughal) stumbled upon close to two hundred settlements from the Mature period of the Indus civilization clustering along the ancient course of the Saraswati (almost all of which, including a city, Ganweriwala, await excavation).

Providential further support for the Hindu nationalist view seemed to come in the form of an excavation photograph from the 1920s showing a broken Indus seal inscription depicting the hindquarters of an animal, accompanied by four characters. Jha and Rajaram claimed that the animal was a horse, as shown in a 'computer-enhanced' drawing published by them; and that the four characters could be read, in Vedic Sanskrit, as *'arko ha as va'*, which they translated as 'Sun indeed like the horse'.[7] The authors translated another Indus inscription, which was discovered in 1990 in Gujarat and is generally regarded as some kind of monumental signboard, as: 'I was a thousand times victorious over avaricious raiders desirous of my wealth of horses!'[8]

But horses were unknown to the Indus civilization, almost all scholars had long maintained, since they were not depicted among the many motifs of animals (including buffaloes) on its seals and in its art, and no horse bones had been discovered by excavators – or at least no bones that convinced zooarchaeologists specializing in horse identification. The bones of the wild ass (onager) are known in the Indus valley, but not horse bones. The horse is generally thought to have arrived in northwestern India only with the horse-drawn chariots of the Indo-Aryan-speaking migrants during the mid-second millennium BC; certainly, in later Indian history, armies imported their horses from outside India. Horses are, however, abundantly mentioned in the Vedic literature. If, after all, horses did feature in the Indus civilization, as Jha and Rajaram claimed, was this not important evidence that the creators of the Indus inscriptions and the authors of the Vedic literature were one and the same – indigenous – horse-riding people?

The arguments in *The Deciphered Indus Script* would probably have been ignored by most people, as had happened with all but a handful of the Indus script decipherments announced since the 1920s by both Indian and non-Indian scholars. But on this occasion, because of their potentially explosive educational and political implications, the book attracted widespread public attention, both in South Asia and even internationally.

Within months, the authors' claims of a successful decipherment were easily demonstrated to be nonsense in articles for national news magazines in India written by scholars, notably Iravatham Mahadevan, the leading Indian expert on the Indus script, Asko Parpola, the leading non-Indian expert, and Michael Witzel, a professor of Sanskrit at Harvard University, with his collaborator Steve Farmer. Mahadevan termed the so-called decipherment 'completely invalid . . . a non-starter'.[9] Witzel and Farmer's chief article was entitled 'Horseplay in Harappa'.[10] They demonstrated beyond question, even for non-specialists, that the supposed Indus alphabet was so absurdly flexible that it could be manipulated to produce almost any translation that the book's authors might desire. Furthermore, the supposed Indus valley horse was revealed – after comparison of the broken seal photograph with photographs of various similar-looking, but more complete, Indus seals – to be a 'unicorn' bull of a type commonly depicted in the inscriptions, not a horse. The so-called horse had to be a hoax image created by one of the authors, an Indian-born, u.s.-trained engineer with experience of computer drawing (and a taste for Hindu nationalist propaganda), as he more or less admitted under questioning by Indian journalists.

Yet, despite the scholarly exposé of this particular book's intellectual bankruptcy, the new Indian government-school textbooks introduced in 2002 referred to 'terracotta figurines of horses' in the 'Indus-Saraswati civilization', and continued to do so until the fall of the Hindu nationalist government in 2004, when the text-books were withdrawn by the incoming government. More important, the idea that the language of the Indus civilization is Sanskrit, and of local origin, continues to enjoy wide support in India, including from some archaeologists and linguists. Until such time as the Indus script is convincingly deciphered, which will not happen without major new discoveries of inscriptions, this heated debate about the Indus civilization's true relationship with the later Vedic culture will surely continue.

That said, the cultural importance of the former Saraswati river, unrecognized in the 1920s, is beyond dispute. In this respect, the Indus or 'Indus-Saraswati' civilization (many archaeologists prefer 'Harappan civilization', after its place of discovery) resembles ancient Mesopotamia, where civilization developed between two rivers, the Tigris and the Euphrates, rather than ancient Egypt, where civilization was the 'gift' of a single river, the Nile. However, the Indus geographical environment was more complex and varied than either Mesopotamia's or Egypt's: a fact that influenced the civilization's evolution more than is obvious from the evidence of its cities alone.

Whereas the city-states of Mesopotamia – ancient Greek for the land 'between two rivers' – remained focused on the areas watered by these rivers, the Indus cities (or perhaps they were

Satellite view of the Indus river showing its course from the Himalayas to the Arabian Sea. The added line in the centre-right section marks the international boundary between Pakistan and India.

city-states) exerted direct control over a far wider area, often through large and small settlements, which supplied the cities with metals such as copper, semi-precious stones and minerals, and timber. Beyond the alluvial plains of the Indus valley, this area may be divided into four regions: the western mountains and pied-mont border zone, the mountain ranges to the north, the eastern border zone and Thar (Great Indian) desert, and peninsular India.

The regions west of the Indus valley are the highlands and plateaus of Baluchistan and along the rugged Makran coast, where an Indus settlement has been excavated at Sutkagen-dor near the modern border with Iran. In the mountainous areas of northern Pakistan, Afghanistan, Tajikistan and Uzbekistan, the civilization established a far-flung settlement, Shortugai, on the northern border of Afghanistan with Tajikistan beside the Oxus river, in order to obtain lapis lazuli from this sought-after mineral's most import-ant mine. To the east of the Indus valley, the ancient Saraswati river was bordered by the Thar desert, which today covers the Indian states of Rajasthan and parts of Punjab, Haryana and Gujarat – all of which contain settlements of the Indus civilization extending almost as far as the foothills of the Himalayas (in the northeast) and the Aravalli ranges (in the east); from the latter mountains the Indus cities obtained steatite (for making seal stones), copper and other metals. East of the Indus delta, in what is now part of western Gujarat, lay the coastal region of Kutch, consisting of many islands in the third millennium BC, unlike today's huge salt marsh, the Rann of Kutch, and the peninsula of Saurashtra – both of which contain many Indus civilization settlements, including Dholavira and a port, Lothal, from which ships traded with Mesopotamia. Beyond Saurashtra, on the Indian peninsula proper, the settlements peter out; yet the Indus civilization obtained large quantities of agate and carnelian from the mines of Rajpipla in hilly eastern Gujarat and possibly gold from far-distant south India.

The climate of this vast area would mostly have been beneficial to agriculture, if we permit ourselves to judge by today's climate. Two different weather systems currently dominate, and sometimes overlap. In the western highlands a winter cyclonic system operates and in the peninsular regions a summer monsoon system – both of which produce rainfall. If one of these systems fails to deliver rain, the other one will almost always do so. Famine is therefore unknown in the Indus valley.

There are six traditional seasons: spring (from the end of February to March), summer (April, May and June), the rainy season (from the end of June to September), autumn (October to November) and the winter and the dewy season (from November to February). These create two basic growing seasons. In winter and the dewy season, archaeological evidence shows that the ancient farmers grew barley, wheat, oats, lentils, beans, mustard, jujube and linen; in summer and the rainy season, millet, cotton, sesamum, melons, jute, hemp, grapes and dates. Rice, which is native to parts of the subcontinent, was probably introduced to the Indus valley as a cultivated crop only towards the end of the Mature period of the civilization, perhaps around 2000 BC.

However, the six seasons, and the two growing seasons, show many variations depending on the region. For instance, on the southern Indus river in Sindh, around Mohenjo-daro, the rainfall is often little or nothing, yet the land is rich in silt deposited by the floodwaters of the river, which compensates for the lack of rainfall. Further north, in the Punjab, where Harappa is located, rain coming from the western highlands in winter and the dewy season can produce, in the spring, fertile harvests and vast grazing. In the highlands themselves, where this winter rain falls as snow, the growing season comes later, with planting in spring and harvesting in summer.

'The juxtaposition of mountains, river plains and coasts provides a unique pattern of seasonally available resources and abundant raw materials that is quite different from the situation in either Mesopotamia or Egypt', notes Jonathan Mark Kenoyer, a key Indus researcher who is one of the recent excavators of Harappa.[11] This diversity of environment, climate and materials must have been vital to the civilization's prosperity. In ancient Egypt, the annual inundation of the land by the floodwaters of the Nile was the single crucial driver in agriculture, and could produce plenty or catastrophe, depending on its level. Irrigation canals were necessary in Egypt to extend the reach of the flood and to store water. In the

Indus civilization, by contrast, there is no evidence for large-scale irrigation. Presumably, if a poor harvest happened to befall one Indus region, rescue was provided by another region with an abundant harvest, by transporting food via established trading networks.

But is it actually safe to assume that today's Indus valley climate applied five millennia ago? After the excavations in the 1920s, Marshall could not make up his mind on this question. In his chief excavation report, he called the climate of the Mohenjo-daro region 'one of the worst in India', with the temperature ranging from below freezing to some 50 degrees Celsius, bitterly cold winds in winter and frequent dust storms in the summer, and average rainfall of not more than 15 centimetres varied by occasional torrential downpours, in addition to clouds of sandflies and mosquitoes. In Marshall's view, 'it will be found hard to picture a less attractive spot than Mohenjo-daro today.'[12] He also noted that the historians of Alexander the Great reported a comparable Indus valley desiccation in the fourth century BC. Could this have developed during the preceding millennium, after the Indus civilization? As part of the evidence for possibly higher rainfall in the third millennium BC, Marshall observed that Mohenjo-daro's builders used kiln-fired, and hence more durable, bricks, rather than more friable, but much cheaper, sun-dried bricks. He also noted that some of the animals frequently depicted on the Indus seal stones, such as the tiger, rhinoceros and elephant – which are not found in the region today – are commonly found in damp, jungly country, unlike the lion, which prefers the dry zone and is not depicted on the seals. But Marshall concluded that none of this evidence was decisive. Kiln-fired bricks may simply have asserted the importance of certain excavated buildings or have been a symbol of luxury, while the disappearance of the tiger from Sindh occurred as recently as the late nineteenth century (probably partly as a result of a reduction in its habitat by increased animal grazing and the effects of big-game hunting). Opinions on Indus climate change remain divided today, after several inconclusive studies. A very recent study suggests there was an abrupt weakening of the summer monsoon about 2100 BC. However, many scholars, including Kenoyer, think that temperature,

'A satanic mockery of snow', Mohenjo-daro. Salination is damaging the bricks, and thereby destroying the excavations, of some Indus valley sites.

rainfall and monsoon patterns have not changed much since the time of the Indus civilization.

Another change to the southern Indus valley was the gradual introduction from the late nineteenth century of artificial control of the river with embankments and dams – notably the barrage completed at Sukkur in northern Sindh in 1932 – and the construction of extensive irrigation canals. These helped farmers, but not archaeologists. Within decades, the over-irrigated land, including the ruins of Mohenjo-daro (now no longer washed by annual Indus floods), became impregnated with salts commonly known as saltpetre. The slightest rainfall would convert the anhydrous salt into the hydrous form, whitening the landscape with 'a brittle shining crust that crushes beneath the step like a satanic mockery of snow', noted an archaeologist at Mohenjo-daro in the 1940s.[13] This process of salination was accompanied by a more than 300 per cent increase in volume of the salt: an expansion disastrous for bricks, which caused the excavated ruins to start crumbling into dust within a few years. At Harappa, there was a parallel destruction of the site by railway contractors and local people in search of bricks for construction purposes. It is fortunate indeed that the forgotten cities of Mohenjo-daro and Harappa were discovered before the Indus civilization became utterly lost to the world, as we shall now see.

TWO
DISCOVERY

Perhaps the most famous statement ever made about the Indus civilization concerns its discovery. In September 1924 an article appeared in the *Illustrated London News* under the byline of the director general of the Archaeological Survey of India, John Marshall. It opened dramatically:

> Not often has it been given to archaeologists, as it was given to [Heinrich] Schliemann at Tiryns and Mycenae, or to [Aurel] Stein in the deserts of Turkestan, to light upon the remains of a long-forgotten civilization. It looks, however, at this moment, as if we are on the threshold of such a discovery in the plains of the Indus.[1]

It had taken a century of significant, but little-understood, discoveries to reach this point. The first hint of the historical importance of Harappa came in the 1820s from James Lewis, an East India Company army deserter, turned explorer, journeying through the Punjab on horseback under the pseudonym Charles Masson. Near the unremarkable small town of 'Haripah', Masson described a 'large circular mound', a 'ruinous brick castle', the remains of buildings on a 'rocky height' and numerous age-old peepal trees 'bespeaking a great antiquity, when we remember their longevity', as he recalled in his 1842 travel account. 'Tradition affirms the existence of a city', an incredible 'thirteen cosses' (some 45 kilometres) in extent, which was 'destroyed by the lust and crimes of the sovereign', added Masson.[2] At this time, nothing was known

Site of Mohenjo-daro, early 1920s, just before the discovery of the
Indus civilization.

of Indian history before the ancient Greeks – not even the date of
the Buddha. Masson tried to relate the mound, and other mounds
in the Punjab, to the various strongholds supposedly captured
by Alexander the Great. But although he came across some unusual objects on the surface of the ruins at Harappa, he found
no treasures.

In 1853 a British army officer and engineer, Alexander Cunningham, while serving in the Punjab, paid the first of what would
be many visits to Harappa. By now, the inscriptions of Asoka had
been substantially deciphered, beginning in 1836, and there was
growing interest in the archaeology of Buddhism. Cunningham
saw himself following in the footsteps not of Alexander but rather
of the Buddhist pilgrim Xuanzang (Hsüan-tsang), who in the
630s made a monumental journey from China through northwest
India to the land of the Buddha in the Ganges valley. Xuanzang
described a great city in the Punjab area, Po-fa-to or Po-fa-to-lo,
with four stupas, twelve monasteries and a thousand monks –

perhaps located at Harappa, thought Cunningham. Unfortunately, he had no opportunity to excavate until 1872, the year after he was appointed as the first director general of the Archaeological Survey. In the intervening period, contractors of the recently established Indian railways plundered Harappa for brick ballast needed to lay the track between Lahore and nearby Multan. By the time Cunningham returned, some massive brick walls that had been present on the site's southern mound in 1853 (which he had taken to be a Buddhist monastery) had simply vanished. Nevertheless, he drew up an accurate site plan and proceeded to dig for antiquities, some of which he published in 1875.

The key find was a seal   the very first Indus seal to appear in print. In Cunningham's own words:

Alexander Cunningham, first director general of the Archaeological Survey of India (1871–85).

The most curious object discovered at Harapa is a seal, belonging to Major Clark [*sic*], which was found along with two small objects like chess pawns, made of dark brown jasper . . . The seal is a smooth black stone without polish. On it is engraved very deeply a bull, without a hump, looking to the right, with two stars under the neck. Above the bull there is an inscription in six characters, which are quite unknown to me. They are certainly not Indian letters; and as the bull which accompanies them is without a hump, I conclude that the seal is foreign to India.[3]

First known Indus seal stone, as published by Alexander Cunningham in 1875, with a modern impression taken from it. The stone is now in the British Museum, London.

Soon, though, Cunningham changed his mind, suggesting in 1877 that the seal was of local origin and written in an archaic Indian script from the fifth century BC, in other words, a little older than the Brahmi and Kharosthi inscriptions of Asoka. He even attempted a translation.

It is not clear how Malcolm George Clerk, an army officer with an interest in Greek numismatics, came by this seal, which Clerk, after sharing with Cunningham, donated to the British Museum in 1892. There it was joined in 1912 by two more seals from Harappa, discovered in the 1880s, in which the characters were recognizably from the same script, in the first case accompanied by a 'unicorn' (rather than a bull), in the second having no animal motif. The first had been dug up by the district superintendent of police, the second by a farmer, who sold the seal to a schools inspector, yet another amateur antiquarian common among British officials in India at this time. In 1912 these three enigmatic Harappan seals were published together in the *Journal of the Royal Asiatic Society*.

And this was not all. Besides the Harappan finds, there was pottery and other objects from sites as far apart as Sutkagen-dor in the Makran and Kalibangan in Rajasthan, discovered during the decades before 1924 and in some cases published in reputable journals. But no scholar was in a position to connect up these disparate discoveries, because the age of the objects was unknown and they lacked any historical context. Like the seals, they were relegated to the status of curiosities. No one suspected the sheer antiquity of Indian civilization: neither Masson nor Cunningham nor Cunningham's successor, Marshall.

Marshall arrived in India in 1902 as director general without the least experience of the subcontinent, at the instigation of that energetic, cultured, imperialist viceroy, Lord Curzon. Aged only 25, he was a classical archaeologist, trained in Crete. Rather than Alexander or Buddhism in India, the Mediterranean region, in particular the Minoan civilization of Crete, was Marshall's initial point of reference. But he soon dedicated himself wholly to furthering the cause of Indian archaeology, despite his department's thinly stretched financial resources.

The scholarly publication of the three British Museum seals in 1912 caught Marshall's attention and therefore played a 'vital role in the discovery of the Indus civilisation', notes Asko Parpola.[4] But perhaps not sufficiently for Marshall to give immediate priority to Harappa's excavation. After further objects from the site, including two more seals, were purchased by one of his assistants in 1912, he noted presciently that 'the excavation of Harappa, when it can be arranged, will be productive of most valuable results and open up quite a new chapter in Indian history.'[5] He authorized some trial excavation in 1915–16; but it fell victim to the exigencies of the First World War and the war's Indian political aftermath: the stirrings of the national movement for independence. When trial excavations by Marshall's assistants finally occurred at Harappa in 1921–2 and at Mohenjo-daro in 1922–3 and 1923–4, their discoveries were as promising as Marshall had hoped.

At Harappa, Daya Ram Sahni dug three shallow trenches into two mounds. Although few structures were found, well-burnt bricks of unfamiliar dimensions were exposed, as were many interesting artefacts such as pottery, figurines, balls, bangles and crucibles – along with two well-preserved seals. Their writing was 'in the same unknown variety of the Brahmi Script' as those in the British Museum, Sahni confidently informed Marshall,[6] who promptly chided him: 'No connection between the Harappan seal-characters and the Brahmi script has ever been in any measure established so far as I know.'[7] Even so, Marshall expressed strong interest in the Harappa excavations in his annual report for the Archaeological Survey, given that Sahni's digging had touched only the topmost levels of the mounds: '50 feet of depth remain to be explored, and it is already evident that the examination of these lower strata is likely to lead to valuable discoveries.'[8]

At Mohenjo-daro – the name means 'Mound of the Dead' in the local Sindhi language – Rakhal Das Banerji became the first person to recognize the antiquity of this hitherto unknown site. He had been preceded at Mohenjo-daro in 1911 by another archaeologist from the Survey, Devadatta Ramakrishna Bhandarkar, who had visited the chief mound in the hope of discovering an impressive Buddhist stupa like those he had spotted elsewhere in

John Marshall, director general of the Archaeological Survey of India, with his wife, officers and staff, 1925, soon after Marshall began to excavate at Mohenjo-daro.

Sindh. But unaccountably Bhandarkar failed to recognize the ruined stupa on the top of the mound and concluded, on the basis of the dimensions and shape of the local bricks, that the ruins were probably a mere two hundred years old, leaving Marshall totally unaware of Mohenjo-daro's potential importance. Banerji, however, immediately recognized the drum of the stupa and began to excavate the stupa's platform. Much more important, in the trench beneath the platform he discovered three seals – the first of their kind to be found outside of Harappa. In early 1923 Banerji explicitly informed Marshall: 'They are exactly similar to Cunningham's Harappa seals.'[9] (He was then unaware of Sahni's seals.)

During renewed excavations at Mohenjo-daro in 1923–4, seven more seals were discovered in a different mound by another archaeologist, Madho Sarup Vats. They, too, resembled those found at Harappa. Vats went on to highlight various other similarities between the excavations at Mohenjo-daro and Harappa in a pioneering letter to Marshall dated April 1924:

It would go a great deal to establish the cultural affinity of Mohenjo-daro with Harappa and their lying in one and the same zone of influence when we remember that not only the size of bricks is the same – viz. 11″ × 5½″ × 2½″ to 2¾″ – but the essential bond between the so-called seals from the two places – the strongest and the most valuable link – as well as the crude caricaturing of terracotta figurines, earthen bangles, balls for slings etc. are found essentially to be of a kindred kind. The cumulative evidence of the finds shows that the site is probably pre-Mauryan [that is, pre-dating Asoka Maurya], though in the absence of a dateable piece, and further and fuller exploration it would be difficult to assign them a definite or even an approximately accurate date at present.[10]

The seals, bricks and other objects from the two sites, such as painted and plain pottery, chert knives and flakes and stone beads, were physically compared by Marshall, Sahni and Banerji at a special conference called by Marshall at the headquarters of the Archaeological Survey in far-off Simla in June. It was quickly apparent to the three archaeologists that Harappa and Mohenjo-daro had to belong to the same culture or civilization. As Marshall put it a few years later: 'One of the most striking facts revealed by the excavations at Mohenjo-daro and Harappa is the complete uniformity of their culture. Though these two spots are some 400 miles apart, their monuments and antiquities are to all intents and purposes identical.'[11] After the conference at Simla, Marshall settled down to write the article for the *Illustrated London News* that would announce this dramatic discovery to the world, with due credit to Sahni and Banerji, three months later.

Banerji thought, strangely, that the new civilization had some distant connection with the prehistoric civilization of Crete, Marshall's training ground as an archaeologist. But Marshall himself from the very beginning maintained that its origin lay in the Indus valley and its surrounding region, notwithstanding his lack of any solid evidence and the fashion in the colonial study of Indian history for attributing all high culture in India to influence from the West, such as that of the Greeks, Romans and Aryans. Marshall's 1924 article boldly concludes that:

this forgotten civilization, of which the excavations of Harappa and Mohenjo-daro have now given us a first glimpse, was developed in the Indus valley itself, and just as distinctive of that region as the civilization of the Pharaohs was distinctive of the Nile . . . The debt which, in the early stages of its development, the human race owed to the Nile, to the Danube, to the Tigris, and to the Euphrates, is already known. But how much it owed to the Indus and the Ganges has yet to be determined. In the case of the Indus, it is probably true that successive migrations from outside had a useful effect, as they did in Mesopotamia and Egypt, in promoting the development of indigenous culture; but there is no reason to assume that the culture of this region was imported from other lands, or that its character was profoundly modified by outside influences.[12]

He was less sure about the date. To begin with, he suggested a tentative 1000 BC at the earliest, some centuries before the civilization in the Ganges valley and the Buddha. However, he rapidly rethought this date within a few weeks of his announcement, following the response to it from Mesopotamian archaeologists. They pointed out seals found in Mesopotamia dating from the early third millennium BC that strongly resembled the newly published seals from Harappa and Mohenjo-daro. Clearly, the new-found civilization must be of the same period, or earlier. In due course Marshall settled on about 3250 and 2750 BC for the flourishing of the Indus cities – a chronology that would in due course be considerably revised by radiocarbon dating in both Mesopotamia and the Indus valley, as we shall see.

The Mesopotamianists' response was also responsible for Marshall's original name for the civilization, 'Indo-Sumerian', rather than 'Indus', reflecting his belief that it might have been strongly influenced by Sumer in Mesopotamia. But in the light of the only Indus excavation he personally undertook, in 1925–6, during which the impressive Great Bath was discovered, and the discovery of a mysterious and sophisticated statuette of a so-called 'priest-king' in 1927, Marshall settled on the name 'Indus', on the grounds that 'Indo-Sumerian' was 'likely to imply a closer connection with Sumer than seems now justified'.[13] The term is used throughout his monumental excavation report, *Mohenjo-daro and the Indus Civilization*, published in 1931.

The influence of Mesopotamia on the Indus civilization has remained contentious. Over the decades, some Sumerologists have gone so far as to claim that the Mesopotamians directly colonized the Indus valley in the fourth millennium BC, whereas many Indian scholars have argued for the spontaneous birth of the civilization in the Indus valley in total seclusion. In between these extreme positions, others argue that the undoubted maritime trade between the Indus valley and the Persian Gulf/Mesopotamia holds the key. For example, Parpola thinks that it was the growth of this trade that 'triggered the process of full urbanisation and led to the creation of the Indus civilisation'.[14] But Dilip Chakrabarti claims that the growth post-dates – rather than accompanies – the beginning of the civilization and 'cannot thus be considered in any way as a catalytic factor in the transformation' from its Early to its Mature (urban) period.[15] Perhaps wisest, if less satisfying, is the caution of Hans Nissen:

> Although it seems almost inconceivable that such [Mesopotamian] influences did not play a formative part [in the Indus civilization], especially as we know for certain that close mutual relations did exist, there is no definitive evidence to show that exceptional features such as seals, pottery, architectural forms, or even the script are derived from western prototypes. These problems cannot be solved with the available material. New evidence for the Indus civilisation in Oman, coupled with further research in the countries between the Indus and the Euphrates [is needed].[16]

Among those who contacted Marshall after his 1924 announcement was Ernest Mackay, a veteran archaeologist then excavating the Sumerian city of Kish on behalf of the Field Museum in Chicago. Mackay had originally trained in Egypt with Petrie, served in the British army in Palestine during the First World War and then worked as a custodian of antiquities for the government of Palestine.

Discovery of
the 'priest-king'
statuette at
Mohenjo-daro,
1927. (See pages
10 and 115 for
close-ups of the
statuette.)

As soon as the extremely busy Marshall realized Mackay's interest
in the Indus civilization, he invited him to take over the excavations.
Between 1926 and 1931, in five seasons of work, Mackay, with some
help from Sahni, dug extensively at Mohenjo-daro, where he revealed
the street plan that gives today's visitor to Mohenjo-daro a sense of
walking through an ancient city. Meanwhile, at Harappa, Vats
undertook eight seasons of work, up to 1933–4, including the excavation of cemeteries and of a complex building that Marshall,
drawing on his work in Minoan Crete, insisted on terming a Granary,
despite the lack of remains of grain (unlike at Mehrgarh). By this

time, however, excavations at Mohenjo-daro and Harappa were forced by budgetary cuts to wind down. In 1931, three days after starting his final season investigating remains to the northeast of the mound containing the Great Bath, Mackay received a telegram from the headquarters of the Archaeological Survey requiring his labour gangs to stop work. Although small-scale work would continue in the Depression years of the 1930s, the big field campaigns at Mohenjo-daro and Harappa were suspended.

In 1944 Indus archaeology received another boost, with the appointment of Mortimer Wheeler as director general of the Archaeological Survey. Wheeler excavated at both Harappa and Mohenjo-daro during his four-year term, using more modern methods than Marshall, based on natural cultural layers rather than Marshall's artificial levels, with constant recording of stratigraphy. Yet Wheeler never published a full report on his work, merely a briefish study, *The Indus Civilization*, in 1953, subsequently updated. All of his writings on the subject are permeated by his long training in the Roman archaeology of Britain, supported by his own military experience as an officer during the First and Second World Wars. In the forthright words of Wheeler's collaborator, Stuart Piggott (who served in military intelligence in India), writing about the Indus civilization in his *Prehistoric India to 1000 BC* in 1950:

> To a British archaeologist the inevitable parallel is the Roman empire supervening upon the prehistoric Iron Age barbarian settlements of his own country . . . the uniform products of the Harappa civilisation can be traced with the monotonous regularity of a highly organised community under some strong system of centralised government . . . There is a terrible efficiency about the Harappa civilisation which recalls all the worst of Rome . . . One can grudgingly admire the outcome of its ruthless authoritarian regime rather as one admires the civil engineering of the Roman army in the Provinces, but with as little real enthusiasm.[17]

Rather than accepting the lack of evidence for violence and warfare in the Indus civilization, Wheeler chose to reinterpret what evidence there was in support of the existence of war, which he regarded as the inevitable accompaniment of civilization. At Harappa, for example, the moment he clapped eyes on the chief mound in 1944, he visualized it as a 'citadel' built to protect the city from attack. Having scraped at the mound's surface and revealed brick lines, he felt his hunch was confirmed. 'A few minutes' observation had radically changed the social character of the Indus civilization and put it at last into an acceptable secular focus', he trumpeted in his autobiography. 'The bourgeois complacency of the Indus civilisation had dissolved into dust and . . ., instead, a thoroughly militaristic imperialism had raised its ugly head amongst the ruins.'[18] At Mohenjo-daro, Wheeler decided that some skeletons found lying unburied in the street levels of the latest part of the city were victims of a massacre by Aryan invaders of the declining Indus cities in the mid-second millennium BC. 'On circumstantial evidence, Indra [the Vedic war god] stands accused', Wheeler famously wrote in his report on his 1946 Indus excavations.[19] Both of these compelling ideas, and others from Wheeler,

Mortimer Wheeler, director general of the Archaeological Survey of India (1944–8), the best-known excavator of the Indus civilization.

would remain influential until the 1980s or '90s, when they were at last overturned by current archaeologists.

'The Wheeler-Piggott paradigm changed Marshall's Harappans from austere, peaceful, perhaps even boring, urban merchant burghers, whose beliefs were harbingers of Indian ideologies, into a people victimised by despotic priest-kings who wielded absolute power from remote citadels, where they safeguarded themselves and the gods who justified their authority', the archaeologist Gregory Possehl remarked in 2003.[20]

Wheeler's term in office as director general coincided with the partition of the Indian subcontinent into India and Pakistan in 1947. The new international border passed through the eastern part of the Indus civilization. This political division had the beneficial effect of spurring Indian archaeologists to search for new Indus sites, for example in Gujarat (where Lothal was discovered in 1954 and Dholavira in 1967) and the northeastern Ganges-Yamuna region (which yielded Alamgirpur in 1958 and Bhagwanpura in 1975). In 1947 a mere 37 Indus sites were known, as opposed to the well over 1,000 sites known today, spread over a vastly increased area of both India and Pakistan. Less beneficially, 'the division of scholarship between the modern borders of Pakistan and India has inhibited the coordination of research projects', notes Rita Wright in her recent study of the Indus civilization.[21] For example, the independent Pakistani and Indian surveys of two rivers, the Hakra in Pakistan and the Ghaggar in India, which flow over part of the course of the ancient Saraswati river, lack a clear scholarly synthesis. Furthermore, there is still no consensus on the terminology and chronology of the various phases of the Indus civilization, especially the transition from the Early to the Mature (urban) period, and its process of decline. However, there is an additional reason for this second lacuna: that the civilization's entire development is now universally appreciated to have been rather less uniform than originally understood by Marshall, Wheeler and the other early excavators of a mere two cities, Harappa and Mohenjo-daro. For instance, the decline in these cities, at the centre of the civilization, was not matched by a decline in its outer regions, Gujarat and the east, where prosperity in fact increased during the

Late period, as revealed by excavations at Rojdi in Saurashtra between 1982 and 1995.

About the civilization's dates there is greater clarity and a consensus, mainly thanks to the invention of radiocarbon dating in the United States in 1949. By the late 1950s there was a radiocarbon laboratory in India, located first in Bombay, later in Ahmedabad. At excavations in Mohenjo-daro in 1964–5 – the last to be permitted there, because of the damage caused by salination – George Dales collected the first series of samples for radiocarbon dating, though he was unable to sample the earliest levels submerged beneath the water table. Thereafter, the technique was used in all Indus excavations having appropriate organic samples available for testing. As a result of radiocarbon dating, combined with a refinement of the Mesopotamian chronology, 'it may now be postulated that the nuclear cities of the Indus civilization were founded sometime before 2400 BC and that they endured in some shape to the eighteenth century BC', Wheeler argued in the 1968 edition of his book.[22] Today, it is generally agreed that the Mature period lasted from 2600 BC to 1900 BC.

The most remarkable site discovered since 1947 is probably Mehrgarh in Baluchistan, located near the Bolan Pass west of the Indus valley, less than 200 kilometres north of Mohenjo-daro, because it has suggested how ancient the roots of the Indus civilization are likely to be. In his 1931 excavation report on Mohenjo-daro, Marshall, so often perceptive in his intuitions, had stated: 'it can hardly be doubted that the story already unfolded will be carried still further back on other sites, of which there are a multitude waiting to be excavated in Sindh and Baluchistan.'[23] Marshall had observed how the explorer Aurel Stein, inspired by the earliest discoveries at Mohenjo-daro, had discovered numerous prehistoric sites in the deserts of southern Baluchistan (the Makran) in 1927–8. Wheeler, by contrast, regarded Baluchistan as some sort of cultural backwater, quite separate from the Indus valley, without any 'direct relations between the two cultural spheres', writes Jean-François Jarrige, the archaeologist who discovered Mehrgarh in 1974 and spent many years excavating the site with his team. '[To Wheeler,] the appearance of cities like

Mohenjo-daro and Harappa seems to have been some sort of spontaneous phenomenon'.[24]

Mehrgarh was continuously inhabited over four-and-a-half millennia from about 7000 BC, and is still the only agricultural site of this antiquity known in Pakistan or India. Its inhabitants lived in houses made of sun-dried brick, stored their grain in granaries, made tools out of copper, used bitumen for sealing baskets, had ornaments of lapis lazuli and fashioned seals made of bone, ivory, stone and terracotta (though there is no evidence for a script). They also created compelling ceramic female figurines with prominent breasts and beautiful, kiln-fired pottery painted with swirling fishes and other animals. But it is the settlement's exceptionally early cultivation of plants and domestication of animals that has attracted the most attention. Was agriculture an indigenous invention at Mehrgarh, or did it arrive by diffusion from the Near East? The current view is that it was a mixture of both. For example, humped zebu cattle become increasingly better represented in the archaeological record of Mehrgarh at the same time as their body size decreases – a trend consistent with indigenous domestication, according to the zooarchaeologist Richard Meadow. Wheat and barley cultivation, on the other hand, which is found at Mehrgarh, has been documented in the Near East of 20,000 years ago.

Mehrgarh appears to have been abandoned after 2600 BC – around the time of the formation of the Indus cities. This raises the question of whether its inhabitants played some role in the cities' formation. The issue is inevitably hard to resolve. However, most archaeologists would agree with Jarrige's claim that there are too many 'direct parallels' between the Mature Indus urban culture and the cultures at Mehrgarh and some other Indus sites of early inhabitation (such as nearby Nausharo and distant Amri, Kot Diji and Harappa) to leave much doubt that in the early third millennium all of these cultures were 'integrated within a vast territory with a remarkably homogeneous material culture'.[25]

How the transition to an urban culture actually occurred in the mid-third millennium is the subject of much debate. Excavation of Early Indus settlements since 1947 shows that more than three-fifths of them were abandoned. Some others were clearly destroyed

Shallow terracotta
bowl with a swirling
fish motif from
Mehrgarh,
c. 2800–2600 BC,
in a style known as
Faiz Mohammad
Grey Ware.

by fire, notably Amri, Gumla, Kot Diji and Nausharo, and then reoccupied. If this burning was the result of warfare, as some scholars suggest (in the tradition of Wheeler), no evidence for weapons has survived within the layer of ash or for violent death in the form of skeletons. Other scholars propose instead that the fires were deliberately started by the inhabitants in order to clear the site, possibly as a ritual act of purification, for rebuilding, so that the new settlement could be planned in an orderly manner.

Whoever may be right about these sites, there is no evidence for burning at Harappa and Mohenjo-daro. Continuing research at Harappa in the 1980s and after by the American-led Harappa Archaeological Research Project, and at Mohenjo-daro by a joint German-Italian team of architects, archaeologists and geologists from the Technical University of Aachen and the Italian Institute for the Middle and Far East (ISMEO) in Rome, has shown that the foundations of Harappa are fundamentally different from those of Mohenjo-daro. Harappa undoubtedly has a long history, predating the Mature period; the city grew organically from a smaller settlement, possibly as old as 3500 BC. Whereas Mohenjo-daro appears to have been constructed later out of nothing on an artificially raised foundation, presumably to protect it from flooding by the Indus river: 'a colossal man-made platform 200 metres broad and 400 metres long, most of which has since subsided down to a depth of 7 metres into the alluvial silt', writes Günter Urban.[26]

Unfortunately, at Mohenjo-daro – unlike Harappa, where excavation has continued up to the present day – it is not possible to examine the deeper levels of the foundations, firstly because of the high saline water table and secondly because excavation has been banned by the government of Pakistan on the advice of UNESCO, which has conducted an international rescue effort, beginning in 1974. The modern research programme at Mohenjo-daro has therefore consisted, firstly, of using the previously unpublished registers of the 1920s excavations to re-examine the site in detail for patterns that may have escaped the notice of the original excavators, and secondly, of applying essentially non-invasive investigative techniques to the ruins.

Thus, unmanned hot air balloons with cameras have taken aerial photographs of the site, which have been compared with aerial photographs taken during earlier excavations. Specially designed 'vacuum cleaners' have removed loose debris from the surface layers of the site to reveal new buried artefacts. Cores have been drilled into the earth to a depth of up to 18 metres and examined to establish times of occupation, types of activities and environmental data. 'For example, household waste dumps were grayish brown in colour, suggestive of fire burning', notes Wright, whereas 'light brown areas and gray areas, especially when mixed with fragmentary bones and tiny pieces of broken pottery, were suggestive of normal household dumping.'[27] As an alternative to drilling, magnetometers have been used to detect subsurface deposits of baked clay, which become magnetized during cooling: a method of detecting buried pottery kilns and burned brick. Instruments that measure electrical conductivity, so as to differentiate soil types by their resistance, have detected two invisible, high-resistance, mud-brick platforms 7 metres long, 6 metres wide and 6 metres deep in the upper and lower town. Even the buried empty street dividing the upper from the lower town has been detected.

In addition to all this, the number of Indus inscriptions available to scholars has continued to expand since 1947. New discoveries have emerged not only from the excavation of new Indus sites, such as the putative 'signboard' found at Dholavira in 1990, but also from the excavation of museum collections in India and Pakistan, where hundreds of seals and other inscriptions had lain forgotten since the 1930s. The *Corpus of Indus Seals and Inscriptions*, edited by the indefatigable Parpola and collaborators, with excellent new photographs to replace the original excavation photographs, appeared in three large volumes, published in 1987 ('Collections in India'), 1991 ('Collections in Pakistan') and 2010 ('Supplement to Mohenjo-daro and Harappa'), with sponsorship from UNESCO. At long last, would-be decipherers have virtually the entirety of known Indus inscriptions at their fingertips.

THREE
ARCHITECTURE

Almost a century after the discovery of the cities of Harappa and Mohenjo-daro, it has become clear that these two sites, for all their importance, do not define the Indus civilization. The many hundreds of Indus settlements discovered and in some cases excavated since the 1940s vary greatly in age, size and complexity. No scholar has yet succeeded in showing that they can be rationalized into a hierarchy, such as that of a large present-day nation with a capital city, provincial capitals, towns and villages.

Harappa is the only major Indus site at which the excavated sequence stretches all the way from the beginning of the Early period (perhaps around 3500 BC) through the Mature period (2600–1900 BC) into the Late period (1900–1700 BC) of decline. Mohenjo-daro is the largest of the five cities, with an area of 250 hectares, and Harappa the second largest, covering 150 hectares, followed by Dholavira in Gujarat with 100 hectares, Rakhigarhi in Haryana with 80 hectares and Ganweriwala in Pakistani Punjab, which is unexcavated but estimated to cover 80 hectares. However, many other sites in India and Pakistan that have yielded important discoveries are very much smaller than these cities, for example, Kalibangan (11.5 hectares), Lothal (4.8 hectares), Sutkagen-dor (4.5 hectares) and tiny Allahdino (1.4 hectares). Not surprisingly, the cities have the most structures, ranging from 'citadels' with walls and gateways and the Great Bath at Mohenjo-daro to streets of ordinary houses with wells, bathrooms and drainage. But even the smaller sites often display significant buildings: Kalibangan and Sutkagen-dor each have a 'citadel'; coastal Lothal has a brick-lined rectangular basin that some archaeologists believe was a dockyard; and unfortified Allahdino boasts a house with three wells of diameter 60 to 90 centimetres. Excavation at Allahdino yielded a jewellery hoard: one of only five major hoards to have been found in the Indus region and comparable with those found at Harappa and Mohenjo-daro.

As for the foundations of these settlements, it appears that even some of the smaller ones, such as Kalibangan and Lothal, were built on anti-flood platforms, like the one at Mohenjo-daro. This platform, constructed out of mud brick faced with a wall of burnt brick, required a massive investment of labour and time. If we accept Possehl's estimate, on the basis that a labourer can move about a cubic metre of earth in a day, the platform at Mohenjo-daro would have entailed four million days of labour. With a really substantial labour force of ten thousand men, the task would have taken four hundred days, or just over a year; with a quarter this number of labourers, almost four-and-a-half years. What drove the labourers, in the apparent absence of any Indus equivalent of the ancient Egyptian pharaoh? According to Marshall, writing in 1931 (though he was unaware of the platform, which was discovered only in 1964 by Dales), 'If there is one fact that stands out clear and unmistakable amid these ruins, it is that the people must have lived in ever-present dread of the river.'[1]

The huge numbers of bricks used to construct these platforms and buildings must have been made locally. But, strange to report, archaeologists have yet to discover any brickmaking sites associated with the Indus cities. Presumably, brickmaking took place in the suburbs or in the countryside, as is typical of modern brickmaking, because of the high temperatures and noxious emissions of brick kilns.

The technical quality of the bricks – both the mud bricks and the burnt bricks introduced in about 2600 BC – is generally high. 'Very few defective bricks are found in the walls of Mohenjo-daro', notes Marshall.[2] But he is less complimentary about their appearance: 'not one of them is moulded or chiselled or shaped in such a wise as to give a hint of any architectural design' – with

An ancient Buddhist stupa stands on top of the ruins of Mohenjo-daro.

the exception of the wedge-shaped bricks in the city's carefully constructed, circular wells.[3] No round brick columns were employed.

The bricks' dimensions were given earlier by Vats in inches: 7 × 14 × 28 centimetres for house construction. A larger brick, 10 × 20 × 40 centimetres, was used for city walls. In both cases the ratio of the dimensions is 1 : 2 : 4.

Was such uniformity the result of a state decree or a federal building code? Probably not, since the ratio, though not found in the bricks at Mehrgarh, pre-dates the Mature period of the Indus civilization. Most likely this particular ratio developed out of experiments by brick masons in order to build structurally sound walls with strong corner joins. 'Scholars originally thought the uniformity of brick sizes represented a strong centralized government,' comments Kenoyer, 'but it is probably the result of concepts of measurement and proportion that were passed from one generation of builders to the next and gradually spread to distant communities along with the specialized artisans.'[4] However, the ratio 1 : 2 : 4 may have held a significance deeper than mere custom and practice. It is also used in the rooms of houses, in their overall plans, in large public buildings and even in the overall plan of the 'citadel' mound at Mohenjo-daro. To Marshall, the effect was deadening, as he explains at the start of the chapter of *Mohenjo-daro* about the city's buildings:

> Anyone walking for the first time through Mohenjo-daro might fancy himself surrounded by the ruins of some present-day working town of Lancashire. That is the impression produced by the wide expanse of bare red brick structures, devoid of any semblance of ornament and bearing in every feature the mark of stark utilitarianism.[5]

The uniformity in construction materials and ratios encouraged a belief among the early excavators that the streets of Mohenjo-daro and Harappa were laid out according to a grid or chequerboard pattern – a surprising regularity for any city of the ancient world. While this is true of the main streets, especially in the lower town at Mohenjo-daro, the detailed picture is more com-

'First Street', Mohenjo-daro.

plicated. In actuality, smaller streets often follow a crooked course, rather than a single straight line, with house walls rebuilt at various angles, although sections of each street are straight and do not curve. City walls, on the other hand, often curve.

Nevertheless, despite these irregularities, the cities appear to have been deliberately orientated along the four main points of the compass. Parpola and some other scholars have demonstrated that this cardinal orientation may have derived from observations of the rising and setting points of certain stars and constellations. For example, according to astronomers, around 2240 BC the Seven Sisters star cluster in the constellation Taurus known as the Pleiades – a crucial constellation in the Vedic, Arabic and Chinese calendars which is also listed in Mesopotamian calendrical texts – rose exactly at the equinoctial point during the spring equinox. To the naked eye, this observation would have held true from 2720 to 1760 BC, a period that encompasses the Mature period of the Indus cities. It would have allowed the Indus builders to establish an east– west line for marking out foundations, a method that is actually set out in a Vedic text dating from around 700 BC.

Thirteen Indus sites have walled 'citadels': Allahdino, Banawali, Chanhu-daro, Dholavira, Harappa, Kalibangan, Kot Diji, Lothal,

Mohenjo-daro, Nausharo, Rakhigarhi, Surkotada and Sutkagen-dor. In some cases the 'citadel' area is located on a mound, as it is at Harappa and Mohenjo-daro, in others there is no mound and the 'citadel' is only slightly elevated above the rest of the settlement but divided from it by walls, as at Dholavira and Lothal. It never lies at the heart of the settlement: it is on the west side at Harappa and Mohenjo-daro, on the south at Dholavira and on the southeast at Lothal. At no site is the purpose of the 'citadel' transparently clear.

Wheeler, primed by his long exposure to Roman fortifications and castles in Britain, instantly visualized the highest of the several mounds at both Harappa and Mohenjo-daro as the ruins of defensive citadels, as already mentioned. At Harappa, he writes in his autobiography, 'The city, so far from being an unarmed sanctuary of peace, was dominated by the towers and battlements of a lofty man-made acropolis of defiantly feudal aspect.' At Mohenjo-daro, 'at once the same phenomenon was clear to see: the flood-worn remains of an acropolis of similar size, orientation and relative position to that of Harappa, and similarly showing the mud or mud brick of which its cliff-like edges were composed.'[6]

The presence of major buildings on these mounds enclosed by walls and gateways, as Wheeler thought, is largely accepted by modern archaeologists (though the walls and gateways are plainer to see at Harappa than at Mohenjo-daro). But it is not understood why separate walls were retained for the different mounds at Harappa, and probably at Mohenjo-daro, so that the city consisted of walled neighbourhoods rather than a unity protected by a single, all-encompassing wall. Since the latter structure would surely have been a more effective protection against attack, this suggests that the walls served a non-defensive purpose and were never fortified with Wheeler's imagined 'towers and battlements'. Indeed there is no solid architectural evidence at all that the walls and gateways were intended for defence. Missing, for example, is any sign of the type of structures found in fortresses in later historical cities, such as a moat or 'a sharp turn just inside the gate to expose attackers to the defenders on the top of the gate', notes Kenoyer.[7] In his view, and that of many other scholars, the Indus cities' walls and gates had to do with controlling trade and commerce between a city and other Indus settlements, rather than with waging war. This would account for the elaboration of the gateways with stairs or ramps and side-chambers, probably to accommodate gatekeepers; for the narrowness of the southern gateway of mound E at Harappa (2.8 metres in width) – sufficient to allow only one cart to pass at a time; and for the existence of a large open space immediately inside the gate, suitable for the detaining of carts and their merchandise by the city authorities. The fact that at Harappa the majority of the stone weights were found inside the gateways lends credibility to this interpretation. The weights were probably used to assess the stream of goods presumably flowing into the city.

That said, there is less archaeological evidence from Harappa for commercial life than we might expect, and especially from Mohenjo-daro, given the excellent craftsmanship of some goods used by their inhabitants. At Harappa, there is certainly debris from kilns and ceramic manufacturing, as well as evidence for copper and bronze workshops, silver- and gold-working and other crafts such as bead making, shell working and ivory carving. But there is no clear proof of commercial facilities, such as shops or a marketplace. At Mohenjo-daro, the early excavators' reports in the 1920s make hopeful reference to the existence of 'commercial buildings', 'shops', 'storage facilities', 'wharves' and even 'public eating places'. But none of these attributions has subsequently been substantiated.

A present-day archaeologist, Massimo Vidale, laments that: 'The most remarkable feature of the industrial organization of Mohenjo-daro is the scarcity, if not the absence, of a wide range of industries of primary importance to the life of the inhabitants.'[8] Were most goods manufactured away from the city, as with bricks? While it is reasonable to think this might be true of pottery making and ore smelting, it seems highly unlikely for advanced crafts like metalworking, jewellery making and seal carving. Both the earlier excavations and the surface surveys of the 1980s revealed some small workshops, some of which contained a furnace, perhaps for smelting and working copper. Presumably there were other, unknown, workshops at Mohenjo-daro, as suggested by the finds at Harappa.

In Possehl's view, 'While it is reasonable for us to believe that there was a rich commercial life in Mohenjo-daro, and this was one of the ways in which the upper classes managed to live in this city, the commercial aspect of Mohenjo-daro does not come through very clearly in the archaeological record.'[9]

Consider the supposed Granary discovered at Mohenjo-daro, and also at Harappa. In the 1920s a structure on the 'citadel' close to the southwest corner of the Great Bath was discovered, containing a number of rectangular platforms of solid brick, each the size of a small room and about 1.5 metres in height, with a series of vertical grooves sunk in their sides. Between the platforms were narrow passages crossing each other at right angles, at the bottom of which cinders and charcoal were found. While admitting that the structure had not been fully excavated, Marshall tentatively identified it as a *hammam*, a hot-air bath, fed by a hypocaust, an under-floor heating system distributing its warm air through vertical flues. But Wheeler, after reinvestigating the structure in 1950, decided it had been a civic granary, in which the grid of air ducts was used to dry the floor of a great timber barn, supported by square wooden beams or pillars, the sockets for which were still visible in the brick platforms. He even identified an external loading

Reconstructed circular brick platform at Harappa. Its original purpose is disputed.

platform for the wagons bringing the tributary corn. Five years later, in his autobiography, he declared with characteristic confidence, resting on his knowledge of ancient Minoan and Roman granaries: 'Set prominently amidst the royal or municipal buildings, this had been the economic focus of the city, equivalent to the State Treasury of later times, register of the city's wealth and well-being.'[10] Today, neither the *hammam* nor the granary theory is favoured. The original excavators found no charred grain or evidence for storage bins – unlike at Mehrgarh; and no sealings of the kind known to have been used elsewhere, notably at Lothal, to seal bundles of goods. 'A more appropriate name for this structure would be the Great Hall, since it was clearly a large and spacious building with wooden columns and many rooms', comments Kenoyer.[11] As for Wheeler's second, rather different, Granary at Harappa, it too founders on a lack of significant evidence for grain or storage bins, plus the fact that a striking series of circular brick platforms nearby, identified by Wheeler as places for grain-husking with a wooden mortar and brick pestle, originally belonged to other buildings constructed at various times and therefore were mostly unrelated to the supposed granary.

Also puzzling, in addition to the dearth of commercial buildings, is the absence of reliable evidence for Indus palaces and temples. Even Wheeler failed to find these! One would have expected the Indus rulers, assuming they existed, to have housed themselves on the 'citadel' mounds, and that their residences would conform to certain elements common to rulers' residences in other ancient civilizations, not to mention the subsequent kingdoms of the Indian subcontinent: in particular, a degree of isolation and inaccessibility to protect the privacy and sanctity of the ruler and his family; private rooms set apart from public rooms intended to receive petitioners and dignitaries; a further area set aside for kitchens, storerooms, workshops, administrative offices and official archives; and, probably, luxuriousness in the private areas. But no such residences have been discovered, whether in the 'citadel' or in the lower town of any Indus city. As for religious worship, there is no shortage of evidence for what may be religious imagery on the Indus seals, in addition to certain objects, such as the 'priest-king' statuette, numerous female figurines and a few phallic objects, which together imply the existence of deities and religious practices. But there are no buildings clearly dedicated to worship – unless we include the Great Bath at Mohenjo-daro. To explain this absence a suggestion by McIntosh may be pertinent. Given the 'humble appearance of shrines' in modern Indian villages, in which worship is generally focused on a tree and a small image, plus the fact that the earliest rock-cut temples in India were modelled on wooden structures, which are of course perishable, perhaps one should not be looking for imposing, brick-built religious buildings in the Indus civilization.[12]

The only large excavated Indus structures of incontrovertible function, apart from private houses, concern water: wells, bathing platforms and toilets, a network of drainage channels and the Great Bath. 'Probably not until later Roman times did people devise so many clever construction techniques to deal with comforts and discomforts related to water', notes Wright.[13] Without doubt, the Indus civilization was the first culture in the world to apply specialized drainage technology to entire urban settlements. And yet one must be a little wary of any temptation to draw a further conclusion, as many have done: that the Indus civilization was uniquely preoccupied with water as a source of ritual purification. But before considering this point further, let us take a look at the water engineering.

The wells of Mohenjo-daro form one of its most prominent features. They were fully excavated in the 1920s, and since they are 10 to 15 metres deep (and still contain water), their brick cylinders now stand up like towers or chimneys. They are also remarkably numerous. One calculation suggests that the city originally had 700 wells, located in both private houses and public areas. Evidence of their regular use is provided by deep grooves in the bricks at the top of the well, which were presumably cut by ropes employed to raise water in leather or wooden buckets, and also by the fact that the wells were rebuilt and their shafts periodically extended in order to reach the water table.

The fact that Harappa may have had only 30 wells begs an obvious question, given that Harappa and Mohenjo-daro were

Wells at Mohenjo-daro, after their excavation, stand up like towers.

not so different in size. Why so few wells at Harappa? One answer is that Harappa probably had more rain than Mohenjo-daro. Second, Harappa may have been nearer to the ancient Ravi river than Mohenjo-daro was to the ancient Indus. Moreover, a large depression found in the centre of Harappa may have been a water reservoir. Undoubtedly, at Mohenjo-daro the Indus represented a threat as well as a boon: not only did it often flood, it also shifted course substantially over long periods, leaving the city without a reliable, river-based, water supply. (Today's great salt marsh in Gujarat, the Rann of Kutch, is the result of a historic shift in the course of the Indus.) 'The architectural solution to the first problem [flooding] was the construction of raised platforms,' writes Michael Jansen, 'and the temporary shortages of water were forestalled by the network of wells.'[14]

Artificial drainage is a defining feature not only of the Indus cities but also of the smaller towns and even the villages. The small-

est drains, constructed of burned brick, channelled effluent from
the bathing platforms and toilets of private houses to medium-
sized open drains in the side streets, which in turn connected with
larger, brick- or stone-covered drains and sewers in the main
streets, supplied with brick 'manhole covers' so that they could be
cleared when necessary. 'Corbelled arches allowed the larger drains
to cut beneath streets or buildings until they finally exited under
the city wall, spewing sewage and rainwater onto the outlying
plain', notes Kenoyer.[15] At this exit point, there may even have
been wooden sluice gates or a grill to prevent intruders from enter-
ing the city by stealth. At Harappa, a completely preserved drain
boasts a corbelled arch 1.6 metres high, 60 centimetres wide and
6.5 metres in length, extending beneath a city street. There are,
however, no true arches of the kind known in ancient
Mesopotamia and Egypt. To Marshall, the absence of the true
arch in the Indus civilization helped to demonstrate that there
was no 'really close connection between Sumer and the Indus valley',[16] given the evident ability of Indus craftsmen to make
wedge-shaped bricks (for lining wells) that would have been suitable
for building a true arch.

The drainage system at Mohenjo-daro was not bettered until Roman times,
two millennia after the Indus civilization.

'The whole conception shows a remarkable concern for sanitation and health without parallel in the Orient in the prehistoric past or at the present day', wrote Piggott in 1950.[17] (His comment resonates the more in India where, according to the government's 2011 national census, 50 per cent of the population had no household toilet and resorted to open defecation.) Nevertheless, this may somewhat exaggerate the effectiveness of Indus sewage disposal, which was not as thoroughly studied by the early excavators as were the marvels of Indus drainage. At Harappa, later excavations have shown that many households had a commode separate from the bathing area consisting of a large jar or sump pot sunk into the floor, which presumably had to be cleared out and emptied into a soak pit rather than being flushed away into a municipal sewer. In addition, Harappa's drains and sewers were clearly not always well maintained by the city's scavengers – about whom we know absolutely nothing – because sewage was allowed to overflow into the houses on either side of the drain. As a result, doorways and walls had to be raised above the level of the street from time to time – as still happens in the modern town of Harappa. Then, after half a century or a century, the ancient municipal authorities apparently built new drains/sewers directly above the old ones.

The apotheosis of the Indus civilization's water engineering is the Great Bath at Mohenjo-daro. Its impressive dimensions, two staircases and watertight construction with bitumen were briefly described earlier, without mentioning that at the foot of each staircase a small ledge with a brick edging runs the entire width of the tank. Hence, people descending the stairs could move along the ledge without immersing themselves in the water.

The Great Bath's purpose was probably not simply public bathing during the very hot weather common at Mohenjo-daro, because just to the north of the tank there is a substantial building containing eight small rooms with conventional bathing platforms. Most likely, the bathing complex was used for special religious functions, in which the water was considered to purify and renew the well-being of the bathers. If this interpretation is correct, it would not be unreasonable to connect the Great Bath with the bathing ghats of Varanasi (Benares) and some other Indian cities, where

Water basin at Lothal, key port of the Indus civilization on the Arabian Sea in what is now the Indian state of Gujarat. It may have been a dockyard.

Hindus ritually cleanse themselves in the waters of Mother Ganges, however polluted those waters may actually be. And yet, there is no definite proof of such water worship in the Indus civilization. 'Of the sanctity of water in the abstract, no tangible evidence has yet been found', wrote Marshall in 1931.[18] This is still the case. 'Water motifs are commonly painted on Indus pottery, but no specific rituals associated with rain and rivers are recorded on narrative seals', writes Kenoyer.[19] Even so, it does seem hard to believe that the labour and skill behind such a large and demanding construction as the Great Bath could have been justified solely by its hygienic function without any underlying religious motive.

The same cannot be said for the very much larger and considerably deeper water basin (22 × 37 × 4–4.5 metres) discovered at the port of Lothal in 1954. Its purpose was clearly utilitarian, rather than religious. But exactly what this purpose was is controversial. The basin was excavated in 1955–60 by Shikaripura Ranganatha Rao, who found evidence that it was the world's oldest dockyard, dating from about 2400 BC. A channel on its north side links it to a river estuary at high tide, while a channel on the south appears to have been an outlet or spillway fitted with sluice gates (grooves survive). Yet, the approach channel would have required a ship to turn twice through 90 degrees, which seems implausible. Nor is the basin close to the port; the two are divided by the river. Its sides are vertical without any sign of access steps. Moreover, its dimensions are on the small side for a dockyard capable of housing several ships. Rao's dockyard theory was quickly doubted, and most scholars now disagree with his interpretation. Perhaps the basin was really a drinking water reservoir or an irrigation tank – but if so why does one of ancient Lothal's drains flow into it, and why does it appear to have been filled with seawater? Like all too many of the large architectural structures of the Indus civilization, the function of the water basin at Lothal, too, is enigmatic.

FOUR
ARTS AND CRAFTS

Compared with its architecture, the arts and crafts of the Indus civilization are well understood. Archaeologists are familiar with its tools and metalwork, carved stone weights, jewellery, shell and stoneware bangles, pottery, sculpture and seals, not only from excavations but also from technical analysis and experimental imitation of the likely processes involved in manufacturing them. These objects demonstrate, perhaps more than the Indus buildings and water engineering, just how sophisticated this ancient civilization was.

Even so, there are unsolved mysteries. The most perplexing is the small size of all the surviving arts and crafts, without any exceptions. Indus art objects always emphasize craftsmanship and technical qualities over monumentality – as in the exquisitely carved seals. To recall Wheeler's perceptive comment, the seals have 'a monumental strength in one sense out of all proportion to their size and in another entirely related to it'.[1] In the entire Indus civilization, there is absolutely no evidence for wall paintings, architectural ornamentation or life-size sculpture, in stark contrast with ancient Mesopotamia and Egypt. The most celebrated Indus sculpture, the steatite statuette of the 'priest-king', is a mere 17.5 centimetres in height. Maybe larger sculptures were created in perishable wood, but if so one would expect their bases or some other fragments to have been excavated. The finest surviving Indus objects – technically and aesthetically – are the elaborately drilled stone beads of jewellery and the seals, both of which found their way to Mesopotamia. But why the artists and craftsmen chose to persist 'in what appears to have been a preference for miniature and less than life-sized art is a puzzle', Dales noted in the 1980s.[2] It has yet to receive a satisfactory solution.

Many Indus technologies appear to have been invented by craftsmen working at or around Mehrgarh before the Mature period of the civilization. Some of the latest Mehrgarh pottery, known as Faiz Mohammad Grey Ware (after its place of discovery on the Bolan Pass), is the equal of any pottery subsequently produced in the Indus cities. Mehrgarh itself has yielded microdrills and other drilling tools used to work beads and various ornaments of semi-precious stone; a lapis lazuli bead was discovered there with a copper rod inside it, which may have been a drill abandoned during manufacture.

The majority of the Indus tools were made of stone: chiefly a very high-quality brown-grey flint or chert from an ancient source in the Rohri Hills to the east of Mohenjo-daro on the other side of the Indus. Several techniques were used to knap and shape the flint core, perhaps the most efficient being inverse indirect percussion, a technique unique to the Indus valley and peninsular India that continues to be practised at the agate bead-making centre of Khambat in western India. Inverse indirect percussion involved the core being pushed at a particular angle against an antler- or metal-tipped wooden stake set firmly in the ground, and then struck with a wooden or antler hammer, so that the stake's tip detached a long, parallel-sided blade from the core. In this way, a single flint core could rapidly yield several blades.

However, some tools were made of metal, that is, copper and bronze, though not iron, which was unknown anywhere in the world until the second millennium BC. The copper was probably obtained from various sources, including Oman in the Persian Gulf and the Aravalli ranges in India. Amazingly, Indus bronze saws must have been as hard as steel, since they were capable of cutting shell as efficiently as modern steel saws. Although no ancient saws have survived, examination of the saw strokes on ancient fragments of shell from Indus workshops has enabled Kenoyer to reconstruct the saw's basic shape. 'It had a very thin serrated edge that was long and curved, similar to the saws still used in shell bangle-making in modern Bengal', he notes.[3] But, interesting to observe, an equally high technical standard was not applied to Indus knives and spears; metal blades went unstrengthened by the midrib required for military effectiveness. Such defective workmanship is generally true of the mass-produced and standardized objects of the Indus civilization, which were 'sometimes quite inefficient', as Parpola remarks, with 'little effort . . . made to improve them'.[4] Why this was so is another mystery, given the competence of Indus craftsmen in more technically demanding areas of manufacture.

For obvious reasons, the standardized stone weights – cubes or truncated spheres made of banded chert, agate or coloured jaspers – do not conform to the last observation. The weights are precisely made, well polished and systematic (though unfortunately not inscribed with any Indus script characters, which would have helped scholars to decipher the script's numeral system). Unique in the ancient world, the Indus weight system does not correspond with any of the weight systems used in Mesopotamia or Egypt. It has left a remarkable legacy in India. It provided the weight standards for the earliest Indian coins, issued in the seventh century BC. It was identical with the system used by the first Gangetic kingdoms around 300 BC (just prior to the reign of Asoka). And it still functions, in the third millennium AD, for weighing small quantities in traditional markets in both Pakistan and India.

The fundamental weight may have been a tiny black-and-red seed known as the *ratti*, which comes from the *gunja* creeper (*Abrus precatorius*) and is used by today's jewellers in Pakistan and India. The *ratti*'s average weight has been found to be 0.109 grams; eight *ratti* would therefore equal the smallest known Indus weight, 0.871 grams. From this basic unit, the first seven Indus weights double in size according to the ratio 1 : 2 : 4 : 8 : 16 : 32 : 64. The commonest weight is 13.7 grams (that is, approximately 16 × 0.871 grams). Thereafter, the system changes from a binary to an essentially decimal one, in which the weights rise in the ratio 160 : 200 : 320 : 640, and after a jump, 1,600 : 3,200 : 6,400 : 8,000 : 12,800 (i.e., in multiples of ten of the binary ratio). 'The largest weight found at the site of Mohenjo-daro weighs 10,865 grams (approximately 25 pounds) which is almost 100,000 times the weight of the *gunja* seed', notes Kenoyer.[5]

Graduated rules, for measuring length, have also been discovered. Of the four known examples, one is made of terracotta and comes from Kalibangan, the second is of ivory and comes from Lothal, the third is of copper and comes from Harappa, while the fourth is of shell and comes from Mohenjo-daro. The length of their divisions is about 1.7 millimetres, with larger units also marked: 17 and 33.46 millimetres on the scale from Lothal, and 67.056 millimetres (the largest unit) on the scale from Mohenjo-daro. It may be significant that 17 millimetres is very close to a traditional unit of length, 17.7 millimetres, noted in the classical Indian 'economics' text, the *Arthasastra*, dating from the fourth century BC or later.

Rules were presumably useful to a wide range of craftsmen, including architects and carpenters. Wood must have been widely used in brick buildings, transportation and other objects, judging from the holes left in brick structures for beams, seal images of wooden boats, terracotta models of oxcarts with solid wooden wheels and metal tools such as axes, chisels and saws, essential for woodworking. But unfortunately no samples of ancient wood have survived. Most likely, cedar and tropical hardwoods were used for buildings and furniture. The cedar, known as deodar (*Cedrus deodara*), which grows in the Himalayas, may have reached the cities via the Indus river and its tributaries. The hardwood was probably Indian rosewood (*Dalbergia sissoo*), also known as sisu and sheesham, judging from cuneiform references concerning the Mesopotamian trade with Meluhha to imports of '*mesu* wood', a term which appears to denote rosewood. Because the heartwood of Indian rosewood is termite-proof, it is still used for making doors, windows and furniture in the Punjab (where it is the state/provincial tree on both sides of the India–Pakistan border).

Wood must also have been used for making looms, judging from various sizes of grooved bricks and stones that were probably loom weights, although depictions of looms are lacking. Textiles were certainly widespread in the Indus civilization, even if only a solitary piece of cloth survives: woven from cotton, it is dyed red with madder. There are multiple instances of impressions left by different grades of fabric on other materials, such as the imprint of rough sacking on the obverse of clay sealings and of jute cloth on a ceramic shard, traces of threads wrapped around the handles of copper objects, the insides of faience vessels originally moulded on a sand-filled bag, and even a toy bed imprinted with some tightly woven cloth made from finely spun thread. Indirect evidence for carpet production comes from the 'distinctive curved copper-bronze knives that are functionally very similar to the curved blades used today for cutting the knotted threads of pile carpets', suggests Kenoyer.[6]

The beads in Indus jewellery were produced from a wide variety of semi-precious stones, as well as from metals – gold, silver and copper – and shell, ivory, steatite and terracotta. Surprisingly, lapis lazuli and turquoise, though valued and traded in this part of South Asia from early times, were not staples of Indus bead makers. They preferred to work with the harder stones – carnelian, agate, chalcedony and jasper – because these retained their high polish, unlike the softer lapis and turquoise. The redness of carnelian (due to the iron oxides, haematite and goethite) was a particular Indus favourite, made by heating yellowish chalcedony packed in a covered pot with cow or goat dung. However, the blue of lapis and turquoise and the red of carnelian could also be imitated, in the first case by colouring beads of faience blue, in the second by painting long terracotta beads with red pigment. These terracotta beads, far less labour-intensive (and no doubt far less expensive) than carnelian beads, make a delicate clinking similar to the sound created by genuine carnelian beads when they are worn as a belt or necklace. 'In modern Pakistan and India, the sound of ornaments is often referred to in poetry to evoke sensual beauty, and the sound of beads and bangles clinking against one another may have been just as important as the visual symbolism evoked by Indus ornaments', guesses Kenoyer.[7]

The hoard of jewellery found at Allahdino contained one of only three known intact belts or necklaces of genuine carnelian beads. It consists of 36 long, drilled, carnelian beads with bronze spacer beads. When discovered by Walter Fairservis in 1976, following

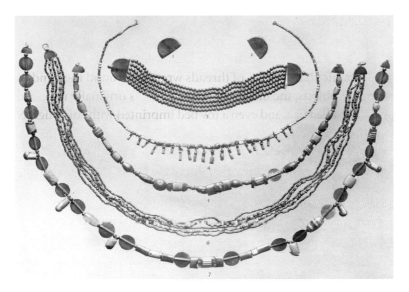

Complete ornaments from Mohenjo-daro, as reconstructed by John Marshall after excavation in the 1920s.

heavy rain on the exposed layers of his excavation, the belt was folded tightly into the centre of an earthenware jar. Stuffed around it were two or three multi-stranded necklaces of silver beads, eight coils of silver wire, fifteen agate beads, a copper bead covered with gold foil and a collection of gold lumps and ornaments. Why had all this been buried in the ground? The collection might conceivably have been the stock of an ancient goldsmith, given that the hoard resembles other hoards found at Mohenjo-daro and Harappa. But this seems improbable, given the very small size of the settlement at Allahdino as compared with those two cities; Allahdino is scarcely likely to have sustained a goldsmith. According to Fairservis's colleague Kenoyer, the hoard of jewellery was probably 'the hereditary ornaments of a woman or her family that had been hidden away for safekeeping' – and never reclaimed, for reasons on which we can but speculate.[8]

Detailed studies of drilled carnelian bead manufacture, both ancient and modern (at Khambat), have been undertaken by Kenoyer and collaborators. The key technological element, the cylindrical drill bit – many of which have survived at sites such as Mohenjo-daro, Harappa, Dholavira and Chanhu-daro – was

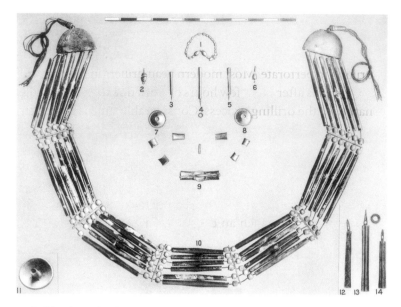

Drilled beads made of carnelian, such as these from Mohenjo-daro, are up to
13 cm long. Each bead required many days of steady, delicate drilling.

made from a rare form of metamorphic rock, modified by heating
to produce an artificial material composed mainly of quartz, sil-
limanite, mullite, haematite and titanium oxide phases. Though
not as hard as diamond, it was the next best thing. It has been
dubbed 'Ernestite' by Kenoyer in honour of the early excavator
Ernest Mackay, who first discovered the material and appreciated
its importance at Chanhu-daro in the 1930s.

Kenoyer describes the likely ancient manufacturing process:

The drilling was probably accomplished by using a hand-held
bow drill, with the bead held firmly in a wooden vice. Because
of the intense heat produced, the whole process of drilling
may have been done under water or with water continuously
dripping onto the drill hole. Drilling experiments indicate
that 'Ernestite' drills could perforate carnelian at a rate of 2.5
millimetres per hour, which was more than twice as effective
as jasper or copper drills used with hard corundum (ruby)
powder. Even then, it would have taken more than 24 hours, or
three eight-hour working days of steady drilling, to perforate

a 6-centimetre-long bead. The beads on the belts from Allahdino and Mohenjo-daro, ranging from 6 to 13 centimetres in length, would have required between three and eight days of steady drilling to perforate. Most modern bead drillers in Gujarat take long breaks after every few hours of work due to the strenuous nature of the drilling process. Considerable time is also taken in the preparation and repair of drill bits.[9]

On this basis, Kenoyer estimates that 480 working days would have been required to make the belt of 36 drilled beads found at Allahdino, from the initial heating of the carnelian to its final polishing.

No wonder, after such an extraordinary investment of technology and time, that such long carnelian beads were part of the

Jewellery was exported from the Indus civilization to Mesopotamia. These Indus-made beads, including five made of heliotrope, were found in the Royal Cemetery at Ur, which dates from 2150–2000 BC.

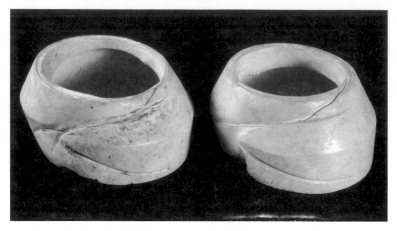

Bangles made of conch shell, from Harappa. Bangle-wearing is still a common custom in South Asia.

treasures found in the royal burials at Ur in Mesopotamia. Some of the Ur beads appear to have been made in the Indus valley, while other beads, judging from their different style, were probably produced in Mesopotamia itself using Indus drilling technology. Presumably, the artisans doing the drilling were migrants from Meluhha to Mesopotamia.

The wearing of carnelian beads must have been a sign of high status and wealth. Bangles, by contrast, were an ornament common to all sections of society and seem to have been important; they are often found in Indus burials. Very likely, this Indus tradition of wearing bangles was one that persisted in South Asia: Indian warriors, for example, wore bangles in battle to protect the wrist and the arm; Indian women wore them to protect their families and ensure long lives for their husbands. The latter custom continues today. From the Indus civilization bangles ranging from simple clay circlets to hollow bangles of hammered sheet gold have been found; white shell and bronze were also used, as was faience, sometimes in imitation of a shell bangle with a stylized 'womb-shaped' motif. But the most prestigious material for bangles appears to have been stoneware.

The technology of stoneware bangles was clearly kept secret and disappeared altogether along with Harappa and Mohenjo-daro, the sole sites of production of these bangles. It first came to the attention of archaeologists at Mohenjo-daro in the 1930s, when Mackay encountered what seemed to be the vitrified remains of an unsuccessful firing of pottery, clay and bangles. Efforts to analyse and imitate stoneware bangle production by Mohammad A. Halim, Vidale and Kenoyer in the 1980s met with only partial success.

The clay they used for the stoneware bangles was prepared as a very fine paste. It was then thrown on a wheel to make a thick, hollow cylinder which, after some drying, could be cut with a cord into bangle blanks, which were allowed to dry until hard. Shaping with a stone blade, burnishing with a smooth stone and polishing with a cloth followed. Finally the bangles were fired at a high temperature inside a clay-coated jar, resting on stacks of terracotta bangles in a kiln closed at the top with a massive clay cap secured with the impression of a 'unicorn' seal. If all went well, the finished bangle was a fine, mottled greyish-black throughout (as revealed by surviving broken bangles) – a result encouraged by researchers' inclusion of organic material, such as goat dung, in the jar.

The most unusual aspect of the stoneware bangles is not, however, their manufacture, but rather their inscriptions and their unexpected size. Every stoneware bangle carries an inscription: a single sign or group of signs from the Indus script traced onto the wet clay before firing. It may be a sacred symbol, a title or even a person's name – there is no way of knowing at present. The diameter of every bangle is 5.5 to 6 centimetres, which is too narrow for it to have been worn around the wrist or the ankle. Perhaps the bangles were worn as a pendant or sewn onto clothing. The headband of the 'priest-king' statuette, and his upper arm, carry a prominent circular symbol that may depict a stoneware bangle. Bearing in mind the characters, the size and the secrecy, 'It therefore seems a distinct possibility that the stoneware bangles were worn as badges of office by leading members of the hierarchy', suggests McIntosh.[10]

Pottery from the Indus cities – both plain and painted – survives in large quantities. The potter's wheel, employed at Mehrgarh, was in use for well over 1,000 years before the Mature period. But the urban Indus pottery is not particularly distinguished. Indeed, the pottery from Mehrgarh, especially the Faiz Mohammad ware, is probably superior to the pottery found at Harappa, Mohenjo-daro and other cities, both in form and decoration. Rather than pottery, the most vital sculpting energies of the Indus craftsman in clay, stone and other materials went into three types of object: numerous animal and human figurines, masks and toys ranging from the frankly crude to the almost sophisticated; a small but significant number of higher-quality sculptures; and, most of all, the thousands of seals.

Many of the female and male figurines appear to have been fertility figurines, judging from their nudity. They were presumably made by potters for worshippers to use in domestic rituals under a sacred tree or in the courtyard of their home. Once the ceremony was over, the figurine was probably discarded or given to children as a toy, rather than being dedicated to a shrine or building (as was common in Mesopotamia), given the figurines' findspots. The animal figurines, which are somewhat more naturalistic and frequently charming and humorous, look as if some were simply toys, while others were intended for worship. For example, a hollow ram's head figurine with a body like a tea cosy mounted on two wheels was assuredly a toy, whereas a finely modelled and incised, hollow, three-headed animal figurine, depicting an elephant with a hollow trunk, with two horns of a water buffalo curving along the cheeks of the elephant and the bottom jaw of a feline with bared teeth at the back of the elephant's head, was probably some kind of cult object.

The sculptures number perhaps ten or a dozen, depending on how one categorizes the finest of the figurines and on the disputed status of two statuettes. The best known of the sculptures are undoubtedly the 'priest-king' in steatite and the 'dancing girl' in bronze, both of which were found at Mohenjo-daro during the early excavations. Neither identification is at all secure. The 'priest-king' (see page 115) is so-called largely on the strength of his commanding face, with its half-closed eyes and closely manicured beard, and the elaborate draped garment he wears, leaving his right shoulder bare – a style that is still considered appropriate in India and the Buddhist world when approaching a shrine or holy

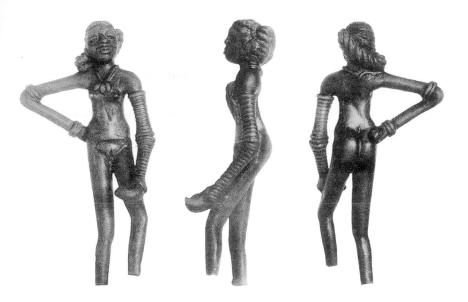

'Dancing girl' statuette made of bronze, from Mohenjo-daro. It is 10.5 cm high, 5 cm wide.

person. In addition, the prominent trefoil designs on the garment, according to Parpola, parallel the trefoils on cloaks worn by gods and priest-kings in Mesopotamia. The vivacious, naked 'dancing girl', confronting the viewer with her left arm sheathed in bangles and her almost bare right arm held akimbo, possibly (but far from definitely) poised in a dance posture, seems still more doubtfully identified. Marshall's comment on her is surely over-confident: 'here we clearly have a dancer or *nautch* girl of aboriginal stock represented, and we may reasonably infer that girls of this class were accustomed to wear nothing more than their ornaments when dancing, though it would be rash to suppose that they ordinarily went naked.'[11]

Yet more problematic, as Marshall was the first to admit, are two damaged statuettes from Harappa: a headless male figure with one leg raised, this time undoubtedly dancing; and a headless male torso. Both cannot help but strike the viewer as distinctly influenced by Greek art, which was a common feature of the art of northwest India in the centuries after Alexander. As a result Marshall, and many subsequent scholars, have questioned whether these two statuettes belong to the Mature Indus civilization, despite the undisputed early provenance of the male dancing figure according to its excavator. The question of their true date remains open, to the extent that the two statuettes are often omitted entirely from current discussions of Indus sculpture.

About the aesthetic quality of the Indus seals there is virtual unanimity. Wheeler's admiration has already been mentioned. Marshall considered the best seals to be 'distinguished by a breadth of treatment and a feeling for line and plastic form that has rarely been surpassed in glyptic art'.[12] Piggott – no admirer of Indus aesthetics, as we know – nonetheless conceded that the seals were 'frequently carved with a brilliant sureness of touch'.[13] Independent India's great artist Satyajit Ray – a graphic designer and illustrator who became a writer and celebrated film director – was so enchanted by the seals that he wrote a short story inspired by the 'unicorn'. Speaking for myself, I first became interested in the Indus civilization after seeing its seals.

Soft steatite (soapstone) etched with a bladed burin like a modern scalpel and then fired in a kiln so that it became slightly harder (about 4 on the Mohs scale of mineral hardness) was the commonest material and process for making Indus seals. The shape was typically square, but it could also take the form of a rectangle, though seldom that of a cylinder, the commonest shape for a seal in Mesopotamia. However, seals were also chiselled, inlaid, painted, moulded and embossed on many other materials: terracotta and glazed ceramic, shell, bone and ivory, sandstone and gypsum, and, rarely, the metals copper, bronze, silver and gold. No doubt the script was also carved into wood, woven into fabrics and basketry, inscribed on palm leaves and perhaps even painted on to human skin. Only semi-precious stones, including carnelian and lapis lazuli, were not used for seal carving – most surprisingly, given that semi-precious stones were often used to make Mesopotamian seals.

On the reverse of a seal was a carved knob or boss, perforated so that it could hold a thick cord. This suggests that a seal could have been worn around the owner's neck or hung from his waist. Larger seals were probably kept in a pouch. It is also common to find that the boss of an excavated seal is missing. It most probably broke off after receiving a knock, as a result of the weakness of steatite combined with flaws introduced in the carving and drilling of the boss, causing the seal itself to drop into the street and become lost. 'Many a surprised merchant must have reached for [his] seal to find a boss with no seal attached', remarks Kenoyer.[14] The loss of a seal would have been a serious matter, but it is not known how the Indus people coped with it; in Mesopotamia a herald announced the loss of a seal, and there were severe punishments for its illegal use. Perhaps this manufacturing defect in the boss is why the seal design was improved in the later part of the Mature period.

We have said nothing about the most important part of an Indus seal: the motif and the script characters. Since these are likely

Seal stones with bosses on the back made of steatite, from Mohenjo-daro. A seal stone probably hung on a cord that passed through the perforated boss and was attached to the seal's owner.

75

to have been connected with each other, and of course with the purpose of the seal, it seems appropriate to discuss them in chapter Ten, devoted to the challenge of deciphering the Indus script. The graphic impact of Indus seal art may be transparent; not so its semantic import.

FIVE
AGRICULTURE

The Indus seals provide clues to the agriculture of the Indus civilization, chiefly through their astonishing range of animal motifs, after making due allowance for the ambiguous or plainly mythical nature of many motifs. So, too, do excavated animal bones and preserved plant remains, such as carbonized grain, and the impressions of stalks and grains in pottery and bricks. Overall, however, the evidence for Indus agriculture is 'extremely patchy', notes McIntosh,[1] as the following three examples illustrate. The elephant is frequently depicted on the seals, and elephant bones have been recovered from many Indus sites (Lothal and Kalibangan, as well as Harappa and Mohenjo-daro, among others), but it is debatable whether the Indus elephant was domesticated or not. Rice was undoubtedly domesticated in the Indus valley later than in the Ganges valley – but it is not obvious from the small amount of evidence available whether rice domestication started before the Mature period of the Indus civilization, occurred during the Mature period, or quite possibly belonged to the Late period of the early second millennium BC. As for grain storage, there is strong evidence for very early grain storage facilities within mud-brick structures at Mehrgarh – but the supposed brick granaries described by Wheeler at Harappa and Mohenjo-daro most likely had some other, unknown, purpose, as we know.

The uncertainty extends to the climate and the river systems, as we also know. While many current archaeologists think that the ancient climate was similar to today's climate, they have no doubt that the Indus and other rivers, such as the ancient Saraswati, have considerably changed their courses and deltas over the past five millennia. How did Indus agriculturalists relate to the ever-changing rivers?

The zooarchaeologist Richard Meadow sums up the relationship as follows: 'agriculture in the Greater Indus Valley traditionally depended not on elaborate artificial irrigation works, but on the manipulation of flood waters and of features of the landscape to contain or exclude them.'[2] In other words, in the valley the farmers may have used simple technologies for water storage and flow regulation and also created embankments to contain water, yet they do not appear to have invested in dams and canals, as the ancient Egyptians did. (On the other hand, such structures might have existed and been obliterated by subsequent erosion and modification of the land.) One such technology was probably the shadoof, an elementary water-lifting device consisting of a bucket pivoted against a counterpoise that was common along the Nile river in Egypt. A seal image from Mohenjo-daro convinced Marshall that it depicted a man operating a shadoof, 'whose counterpoise is seen at the end of the pole above and behind his head'.[3] Probably he was right, although the seal drawing is decidedly sketchy. Certainly, outside the Indus flood plains, dams and reservoirs were used to slow down water, trap runoff and store water. In the hills of Baluchistan, evidence exists of dam-like stone structures known as *gabarbands*, which were constructed about halfway across hill torrents and small rivers in order to capture both soil and water. At Dholavira there is a sophisticated, stone-built water conservation system consisting of channels and reservoirs, one of which is more than 5 metres deep with a series of 31 steps leading from top to bottom. Perhaps the so-called dockyard at Lothal was another such reservoir.

Freshwater fishing in the rivers was probably commonplace, unsurprisingly. Copper fishhooks have been excavated from many houses. Fishing nets, too, were used, as depicted on a potsherd from Harappa; the nets were weighted with terracotta sinkers, which have been found in settlements ranging from cities to villages. Saltwater fish, caught on the coast, were transported – presumably in dried form – as far inland as Harappa, where their bones have been discovered in considerable quantities.

Crops were grown when the heaviest flooding of the rivers had receded, during two basic growing seasons – the winter and dewy season, and the summer and rainy season (monsoon) – as discussed earlier. In some places the ground was fertile enough for seed to be broadcast without prior preparation; in others ploughing was required. No ploughs survive, but their existence is strongly suggested by a terracotta toy plough found at Banawali and a miniature clay yoke discovered at Nausharo, not to mention terracotta models of carts pulled by bullocks. Moreover, studies of cattle bones indicate pathologies characteristic of the type of physical stress caused by traction for transport and ploughing. There is also the remnant of a ploughed field found at Kalibangan – the world's earliest-known ploughed field – that corresponds with a method of ploughing still used in the region. The field was first ploughed in narrow strips in one direction, and then in wider strips at right angles to the first direction. The seed planted today in the narrow strip is horsegram (a variety of bean) and in the wider strip mustard – the second of which was grown in the Indus civilization, though there is no evidence that mustard was the crop planted in this ancient Kalibangan field.

The wide variety of Indus crops was mentioned earlier, too. Not all of these were cultivated during the same period, however. Agriculture in the Mature period concentrated on wheat, barley and pulses – that is, the West Asian group of domesticated crops, grown across an area from western Europe to the Indus area. At the very end of this period, or during the Late period, new crops – several varieties of millet and also rice – came under cultivation, although it is possible that these new crops were cultivated in Gujarat earlier than this, as early as the beginning of the Mature period. Millet and rice were more suited than wheat and barley to a monsoon climate, since they could be planted after flooding. They changed the productivity of some areas that were already under cultivation and brought new areas under cultivation.

Millets, supposedly originating in Africa, were cultivated in Arabia during the fourth millennium BC, from where they eventually made their way to the Indus area, via the Indus trade with Oman. Today, they are known in the Indian subcontinent by their

Votive objects made of terracotta, including zebus (humped bulls) and a wheeled cart, from Harappa.

Hindi-Urdu names: *jowar* (sorghum, *Sorghum bicolor*), *bajra* (pearl millet, *Pennisetum typhoideum*) and *ragi* (finger millet, *Eleusine coracana*). As Possehl explains:

> The importance of these [millets] is that they are summer grasses that prosper during the southwest monsoon, unlike wheat and barley, which are winter grasses that do not thrive as monsoon crops. The millets thus led to double or year-round cropping and were important, if not critical, additions to the prehistoric food supply.[4]

The beginning of rice cultivation is more obscure, as remarked. Indeed, many books on the Indus civilization, including Marshall's 1931 study *Mohenjo-daro*, do not mention rice, or mention it only in passing, because the evidence for its cultivation is deemed to be too slight. A complicating factor is that rice is indigenous to parts of South and East Asia, including the Indus area and the Ganges valley; in other words, it grew wild there, before it was

A bullock-cart from the Indus valley.

domesticated. In Gujarat, at Lothal and Rangpur, Indus pottery has revealed charred rice husks and impressions of rice husks and leaves. But, according to studies by at least one scholar, Naomi Miller, this fact probably does not suggest the presence of rice domestication. Miller thinks that the rice in question was wild rice, which had been eaten by grazing cattle, excreted in their dung and then burned by people as fuel or used as a tempering agent in the firing of pottery.

The domestication of rice probably involved a number of different centres. On the basis of genetic evidence, it happened in at least two areas of Asia: 'a perennial wild rice in East Asia produced the short-grained *japonica* variety', whereas in South Asia, 'an annual wild rice gave rise to the long-grained *indica* variety, which also spread through Southeast Asia and China', according to McIntosh.[5] The South Asian development may have occurred as early as 5000 BC in the Ganges valley, 'if not earlier', argues Chakrabarti, but it was definitely underway by the third millennium BC.[6] Yet it is not at all clear how or when rice domestication got going in the Indus valley, and whether it was influenced by domestication in the Ganges valley. 'The evidence for rice as a crop is limited in the Indus region as a whole,' McIntosh cautiously writes, 'though it may have been present at Harappa' – where rice husks have been found in pottery and bricks.[7] Its domestication could conceivably have started with the sowing of wild rice in the wetlands created by Indus flood water retained in valley depressions, rather as today's rice farmers take advantage of the margins of the artificial Lake Manchar, a fluctuating body of water located west of the Indus and created in the 1930s by the construction of the Sukkur Barrage. However it was that domestication actually began, the earliest unequivocal occurrence of cultivated rice, of the *indica* variety, seems to belong to an eastern Indus site, Hulas, in the Ganges-Yamuna region, dating from the end of the Mature period (2000 BC or later).

Animal life in the Indus civilization was abundant, judging from the seal motifs, painted imagery on pottery, terracotta figurines and fossil bones. Among real species, the seals depict the humped bull or zebu (*Bos indicus*), the non-humped bull (*Bos taurus*), the

Indus seal stone made of steatite with a zebu (humped bull) motif, from Mohenjo-daro.

water buffalo (*Bubalus bubalis*), the gaur or Indian bison (*Bos gaurus*), the Indian rhinoceros (*Rhinoceros unicornis*), the tiger (*Panthera tigris*), the Asian elephant (*Elephas maximus*) and the gharial, a fish-eating crocodile (*Gavialis gangeticus*). Not included in the seal motifs, but depicted in other art, are the bear, dog, hare, monkey, parrot, peacock, pig, ram, squirrel and some birds too roughly portrayed to be definitely recognized. For example, a model in pottery from Mohenjo-daro with a long and wide-spreading tail and eyes represented by oval pellets may be a peacock, a creature plainly painted on pottery from Chanhu-daro. (Meluhha is said in cuneiform sources to have been a land of '*haia*-birds' with cries able to 'fill the royal palaces' – probably peacocks.) The goat is surprisingly under-represented, though it does appear in its wild form as the ibex and the markhor, sporting easily identifiable horns. Not depicted at all, either in the seal motifs or in other art, are horses and camels. A puzzling, one-horned animal is very frequently depicted on the seals (over 60 per cent of the Mohenjo-daro seals and around 46 per cent of the Harappan), and is also modelled in several one-horned terracotta figurines (from Harappa, Mohenjo-daro and Chanhu-daro). It is generally termed a 'unicorn', a creature legendarily associated with India by ancient Greek writers; its zoo-logical identity, if it actually existed, is much debated. In Marshall's view, its lack of naturalism in the seals suggested the 'unicorn' was a mythical creature.

Cattle, goats, sheep and dogs had undoubtedly been domesticated. Cattle – that is, the humped zebu, the non-humped bull and the water buffalo – were the most important of the domesticated animals. 'These distinctive species were adapted to different habitats and were probably used in different ways by the Indus people', argues Kenoyer, basing his view on the marked varieties of hump and horn displayed by Indus figurines of cattle, combined with observations of cattle in the present-day Indus area and how they are used. He explains:

> Several breeds now found in the greater Indus valley result from selective breeding and geographic adaptation that may have begun during or even before the period of the Indus cities. Large humps and medium-length horns are characteristic of the cattle found in the central plains, while in Gujarat and parts of Sindh, the cattle are distinguished by smaller humps and wide, spreading horns. Both varieties are well adapted to the heat, and their lumbering gait is effective in pulling ploughs or oxcarts. The smaller non-humped cattle and a range of cross-breeds are found along the foothills and highland regions, where they easily graze on the rocky slopes. Because of their adaptability to the highlands, these species would have been useful pack animals, carrying much more than the twenty-kilogram average for human porters.[8]

The water buffalo, by contrast, inhabits the marshy land near the rivers, suitable for wallowing in mud, as required by its relatively hairless skin. Although it, too, might have been used for pulling carts and ploughing, it was probably used more for milk production, judging from current agricultural practice in an area around the Ravi river not far from Harappa. Sahiwal has long been noted for its breed of water buffalo, which produces milk with a higher fat content than cow's milk. Sahiwal buffaloes may have been famous in the days of ancient Harappa, too.

The domestication of goats (*Capra hircus*) and sheep (*Ovis aries*) is clear from the bones of both species discovered at various sites. At Harappa, goat remains are relatively rare, whereas sheep remains are plentiful. The large size of the sheep bones suggests that the animals were bred to produce meat and wool, according to Kenoyer. However, direct evidence for Indus wool production from goats and sheep is lacking. For example, the surviving impressions of vanished textiles mentioned earlier do not include wool; nor are woolly sheep and woollen textiles ever depicted in the Indus area, as they are in Mesopotamia; nor have any combs (for removing wool from sheep) or spindle whorls (for spinning wool) been discovered, as they have been in Europe. Additionally, analysis of sheep remains from the coastal Indus settlement of Balakot indicates that most male sheep were culled young, before the best age for wool production. Possibly the Indus civilization did use wool but preferred to import it from Mesopotamia.

Dogs (*Canis familiaris*) were part of Indus households, judging from the occurrence of their bones and from dog imagery. The bones of a dog unearthed in a house at Mohenjo-daro led zoologists to conclude that: 'the remains are those of one of the domestic or semi-domestic dogs that are common at the present day around every Indian village, and at the present time live around the site of the excavations', according to Marshall's 1931 report.[9] Dog figurines often wear collars. One such is clearly a pet dog, another is a performing dog in the act of begging, yet another a fighting dog, and a fourth may be a retriever for hunting, since it has a kill in its mouth. It could be that Indus hunters captured, trained and even exported wild red dogs, which are celebrated hunters, since cuneiform texts refer to a 'spotted dog' or a 'red dog' from Meluhha. A brick from Chanhu-daro, which must have been laid

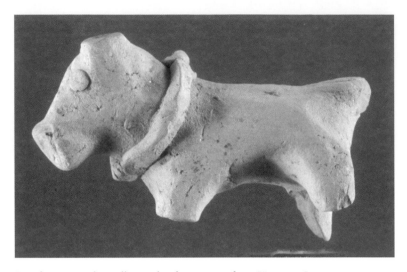

Dog figurine with a collar made of terracotta, from Harappa. It suggests domestication.

out to dry in the sun, carries a trail of paw prints of a dog pursuing a fleeing cat. Whether or not cats, as well as dogs, were domesticated, is unclear.

Elephants must have been hunted for their meat and their ivory, which was carved into ornaments, gaming pieces and inlay. In the seal motifs and in other imagery, elephants are always depicted without human riders, which perhaps suggests that they were not employed for heavy labour, unlike in historic India. Yet, one seal does show an elephant with a cloth on its back (a caparison?), while a lively terracotta figurine of an elephant's head from Harappa – perhaps a toy or a puppet – bears traces of coloured paint: red-and-white bands across its face. This decoration is reminiscent of the present-day Indian custom of painting the faces of elephants, especially for festivals and religious processions. So it is possible that Indus elephants were domesticated, too.

The earliest definite evidence for the domesticated horse (*Equus caballus*) in the Indian subcontinent comes from the Punjab in the period between 1700 and 1500 BC, post-dating the disappearance of the Indus civilization, according to most archaeologists. A few researchers, mostly from India, including Chakrabarti and S. P. Gupta, argue for the horse's earlier presence during the Mature period. The issue is controversial, as we already know, because of its political connotations for Hindu nationalists. While there is definitely no imagery of horses from the Mature period, it is at least conceivable that there are bones of horses. But Meadow's detailed studies of equid bones from the Mature period and before indicate that the bones are most probably those of the onager, also known as the steppe ass (which resembles a donkey to untutored eyes). This wild equid, *Equus hemionus*, is native to northern South Asia, unlike *Equus przewalskii*, the ancestor of *Equus caballus* (the domesticated horse), which is indigenous to the steppe region from Ukraine to Mongolia. 'Morphologically, the two species are similar and it is often difficult to distinguish their bones', notes McIntosh.[10]

We now have a picture of the plants and animals available for consumption by the Indus civilization. How did its people prepare them as food? Unfortunately, the evidence is very thin. There are few remains of ancient vegetables, for instance, and 'no representations of elaborate feasts are preserved', as Kenoyer remarks.

Head of an elephant figurine made of terracotta, from Harappa It bears traces of coloured paint across its face, reminiscent of the contemporary South Asian custom of painting the faces of elephants.

South Asian steppe asses, or onagers. The steppe ass resembles a donkey in appearance, while its bones, which have been found at Indus sites, resemble the bones of the ancestor of the domesticated horse.

Reconstruction of Indus meals must therefore depend on what is known to have been available in the cities' markets, plus information about vegetables, fruits, nuts, honey and so forth known to be indigenous to the Indian subcontinent.

Kenoyer guesses that: 'Wheat probably was the foundation for most meals, but other staple dishes would have been made from roasted barley, stewed or fried lentils, gram (chickpea) flour, baked tubers and various wild grains' – perhaps including wild rice. 'Meat preparations would have been grilled and roasted, stewed or fried and even minced with various herbs and spices.'[11]

Exactly what those herbs and spices were can only be conjectured on the basis that basil, coriander, garlic, onion, ginger, turmeric, cinnamon, fenugreek and cumin grew wild in north India, whereas cloves, cardamom, nutmeg and various types of black pepper grew primarily in south India. But we should not assume that these latter, sought-after spices – which are mentioned in the later Vedic texts – were unavailable to the Indus area during the third millennium BC. Long-distance trade is a remarkable, if somewhat underappreciated, fact of the ancient world – whether in the Mediterranean area, Mesopotamia or Asia as a whole. If Meluhha could successfully trade with Mesopotamia at this exceptionally early period (as it unquestionably did), then it is possible that south Indian spices were available at Indus settlements near the coast such as Lothal and Dholavira, which enjoyed easy access via the Arabian Sea to the coasts of the Indian peninsula. Conceivably, even inland at Harappa and Mohenjo-daro, Indus cooks spiced their dishes with such exotic subcontinental imports.

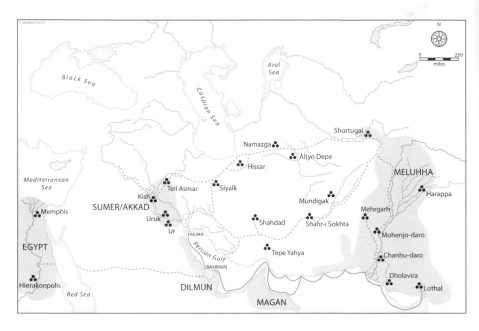

Map showing trade routes of the Indus civilization by land and sea.

SIX
TRADE

Trade in the Indus civilization was an exceptionally far-flung enterprise. Goods were transported to the cities from their hinterlands and neighbouring lands by both road and boat, but only after the close of the annual monsoon rains, when landslides ceased in the mountains, swollen flood waters receded in the plains and muddy roads dried out, becoming passable for animals and men. In the Indus valley itself, heavy goods were moved on the flat by long lines of carts hauled by zebu cattle, while porters carried lighter goods in baskets suspended from the ends of a long wooden pole. From the highland plateaus west of the valley came caravans of pack animals – oxen, sheep and goats (but no camels or horses) – carrying copper, precious stones, wool, fruit and nuts. In addition, there was long-distance trade with areas of Baluchistan further to the west and the Aravalli ranges of Rajasthan to the east (both of which were sources of copper), with coastal Gujarat and the Makran coast (sources of marine shell), with northern Maharashtra (where carnelian was mined) and with Afghanistan (the chief source of lapis lazuli), and still further afield, by ship, with the Persian Gulf and Mesopotamia, where Indus jewellery, weights, seals and other objects have been excavated. Around 2300 BC the Akkadian ruler Sargon boasts in a cuneiform inscription of ships from Dilmun, Magan and Meluhha docking at his capital Akkad (Agade), somewhere east of the Tigris river. Dilmun appears to refer to modern Bahrain, Magan to modern Makran and Oman, Meluhha to the Indus valley region.

Indus trade networks carried a product to places far from its source. Marine fish from the south coast in Gujarat reached Harappa, as already mentioned. Carnelian from northern Maharashtra has been found in Chanhu-daro, Mohenjo-daro, Harappa and as far north as Shortugai on the northern border of Afghanistan – and, of course, in Mesopotamia. The fact that many raw materials, such as copper, steatite and shell, came from not just one but several sources encouraged the networks to develop and expand, stimulating economic competition and growth. It is difficult to contemplate the challenges and discomforts these anonymous traders must have faced four to five thousand years ago, as they voyaged across major rivers, mountains, deserts and even the ocean. Average Indus dwellers – especially those who lived in rural areas – no doubt ventured little further than a few kilometres from their homes, to work in the fields, to look after animals and to cut wood for cooking and construction purposes. But they probably witnessed long-distance travellers returning to distant towns or embarking on a journey of hundreds of kilometres from one of the major population centres.

For example, Shortugai, on the Oxus (Amu Darya) river, was more than 600 kilometres from Harappa, almost 1,000 kilometres from Mohenjo-daro and some 1,500 kilometres from the port of Lothal. Yet it was a full-fledged settlement, in effect an Indus colony. 'None of the standard attributes of a Harappan complex is missing', writes Maurizio Tosi.[1] Shortugai's excavators, who located the site in 1976, discovered carnelian and lapis lazuli beads, bronze objects, terracotta figurines and models of carts, shell bangles and a seal with a rhinoceros motif. The bricks in the houses have the characteristic Indus dimensions. A ploughed field with flax seeds, and irrigation canals, indicates the existence of farming. Yet, the *raison d'être* of Shortugai, judging from its outlying location, was probably not standard. It seems to have been founded as a trading post for products from the mines of northern Afghanistan: mainly lapis lazuli but also metals, including gold.

How were such extensive trade networks controlled and operated? There is no evidence for any Indus coinage; and in the absence of an agreed decipherment, no sign in the script can be allotted to a

Seal impression on a clay tag with an elephant motif, from Lothal. It was preserved in a fire.

currency, unlike in the Sumerian script, where the 'axe' pictogram stands for *gin,* a Sumerian word that refers to both an axe and a monetary unit, the shekel. However, there is some solid, if ambiguous, evidence for the control of the Indus trading system from seal impressions and weights, and clearer evidence for its methods of transport from both imagery and other sources.

At Lothal, more than a hundred seal-impressed clay tags were found by archaeologists. They were preserved as a result of being baked in a fire that burned down a large house nearby. The most frequent motif in these seal impressions is the unicorn, followed by the elephant and some swastikas. But what is most revealing is that many of the clay tags have been stamped with more than one seal, in some cases with four different seals. Usually, each new impression has obliterated the animal motif of the previous impression, but in certain cases the overlapping impressions apparently repeat the unicorn motif, visible in the tip of its horn along with the characters of the script. These multiple sealings suggest two different possible interpretations regarding the organization of the Indus trade, according to Kenoyer. Either different owners – up to four of them – were involved in a single commercial transaction, or several (customs?) officials were required to check and approve the contents of a bundle of goods before it could be exported or imported.

With the weights, the common-sense interpretation is that the lighter weights must have been used in everyday commercial transactions for weighing precious stones, metals, perfumes and other highly valuable items, while the heavier ones were applied in weighing large quantities of goods, such as grain. However, this simple view founders on the fact that too few weights have been discovered at the Indus settlements, observes Kenoyer, who argues for weights as an instrument in taxation, as follows:

> In the recent excavations at Harappa, the highest concentration of weights has been found inside the city gateway, which is where goods coming into the city would have been weighed and taxed.

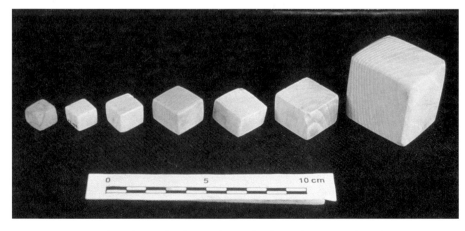

Seven cubical weights made of chert, from Allahdino. The system of weights implies a sophisticated economy.

Tax collectors or village elders in the smaller settlements would have needed only one or two sets of weights to collect tribute in precious commodities or produce. Finally, the large weights which are found only at the urban centres would have been well suited for weighing tribute coming from all of the surrounding villages and towns.[2]

Turning to methods of transport, it is possible to infer the design of the oxcart used in the plains from both ancient toy carts and present-day Indus carts. Toy carts made of terracotta vary somewhat in design: some have solid floors and sidebars, while others have hollow frames and removable sides fitting into holes. All of the real carts must have been made from wood, probably with harnesses made from leather and sinew. The heavy axle and the solid wheel probably rotated as a single unit like the traditional oxcarts still used in Sindh, suggests Kenoyer: 'This simple construction is quite well adapted to the wide sandy plains, where wide turns are the norm and a squeaking axle does not bother anybody.'[3] The original wheel span was 1.6 metres, judging from the cart tracks preserved in the streets of ancient Harappa. The cart could probably carry about 1,870 kilograms of cargo.

As for boats, it is inconceivable that they did not exist – bearing in mind the maritime trade between the Indus area and Mesopotamia – and yet no archaeological remains of boats have been found thus far, presumably because they were constructed of perishable materials and kept by the riverside, not in town. However, there are clay models of river boats from Harappa, and two striking images of boats on a steatite seal and a terracotta amulet from Mohenjo-daro. These resemble the shape of the traditional, wooden, flat-bottomed houseboats seen today on the Indus in Sindh, with a cabin on the deck, a high bow, a high stern and a pair of steering oars or paddles, suitable for transporting goods in shallow waters without the need for a quay or dock, but no sail, despite the existence of suitable sail-making fibres (such as cotton) in the Indus civilization. Nevertheless, the hull appears to be made of reed (rather than wood), according to the excavator of the steatite seal, Mackay – though in truth the seal image in question is not clear enough to be certain. If reeds really were the basic construction material, they may have been in bundles lashed with cords, perhaps using baru grass (*Sorghum halepense*), a local plant used for boatbuilding in present-day Gujarat. Furthermore, they may have been caulked with bitumen to make them waterproof (like the bricks of the Great Bath at Mohenjo-daro), although there is no evidence for the use of bitumen on any Indus boats. The practice has been found at various sites along the Arabian peninsula, but bitumen was not used in South Asian ship construction during recorded times. Without bitumen, a reed boat would have lasted only a few months before starting to rot – a further reason for the lack of preserved boat remains.

To what extent such a reed-made river vessel would have been seaworthy is debatable. In 1977–8 the adventurer Thor Heyerdahl proved that a reed boat (*Tigris*) – which he built in Iraq, sailed to the Indus delta in Pakistan, sailed back to the Red Sea and then jettisoned in Djibouti on the coast of Africa – could remain sea-

Boats as depicted on an unfired steatite seal stone (top) and a terracotta amulet (bottom), from Mohenjo-daro. The boats have high prows, a central cabin and a double rudder; the boat on the amulet also has birds on deck.

Houseboat with a sailing mast on the Indus river near Mohenjo-daro, 1971.

worthy for at least five months. Heyerdahl was convinced that the Indus boat depicted in Mackay's steatite seal demonstrated 'cross-lashings characteristic of a reed-craft'.[4] He did not use bitumen on the *Tigris*, after experiments in the Tigris river showed that bitumen did not prevent waterlogging of the reeds and simply added to the boat's weight. Almost certainly, the Indus dwellers learned what journeys were feasible with their boats by navigating them through the numerous creeks and waterways of Kutch. After this, they probably learned to voyage under sail along the Makran coast to the Persian Gulf and thence to the cities of Mesopotamia, whence they retraced their steps with a new cargo, trading all along the route: a process of coastal navigation and trade that continued until the modern period, known as cabotage. 'They travelled in short hops, following the same routes year after year, staying ashore when the southwesterlies blew strong, coasting east and west close inshore when the gentle northeasterlies returned', writes the maritime historian and sailor Brian Fagan.[5] Only very much later, in the second century BC, did sailors and merchants learn how to sail over the open ocean from the Red Sea to India and back on an annual basis using the southwest and the northeast monsoons. If the pioneering sailors of the Indus civilization got too far away from the Makran coast, they may have received navigational help from birds, two of which are graphically depicted on the deck of the flat-bottomed boat in the Mohenjo-daro amulet. A bird (maybe a crow) would have been released into the sky, so that it might fly in the direction of the nearest land.

Did the flat-bottomed Indus river boats mutate into the crescent-shaped hull of Heyerdahl's reed boat before taking to the Arabian Sea? Did they reach as far as the coast of East Africa, as the *Tigris* did? No one knows. But it is suggestive that the millets introduced into the Indus area via Arabia during the third or early second millennium BC supposedly originated in Africa; possibly they were originally foodstuffs given to boat crews returning from East Africa to the Persian Gulf. And it is intriguing that the supposed Mesopotamian name for the Indus area during the third millennium and early second millennium, Meluhha, was reassigned to Ethiopia by the fifteenth century BC, following the decline of the Indus civilization. What is relatively certain is that the initiative for the maritime trade between the Indus area and Mesopotamia came from the Indus people, not the Mesopotamians. For there is no evidence that Mesopotamian boats sailed – like Heyerdahl's *Tigris* – from Mesopotamia as far as Meluhha in the mid-third millennium BC; the boat traffic along the Makran coast commenced in the opposite direction. As McIntosh observes, 'the fact that Indus merchants are known to have travelled to Mesopotamia, while Mesopotamian ships did not venture outside the confines of the [Persian] Gulf, suggests that the development of seaworthy vessels was an Indus innovation.'[6]

The archaeological evidence found in Mesopotamia for the existence of this trade is unequivocal, but also problematic. It consists principally of carnelian beads (drilled and etched), weights and seals, all of which are easily identifiable with the Indus civilization.

Thus, a weight made from yellow carnelian found at Ur in Mesopotamia is a cube 1.85 × 1.85 × 1.80 centimetres with slightly bevelled corners weighing 13.5 grams, that is, very close to the most common weight at Indus sites. 'Its material, shape, and weight leave no doubt that it is an [Indus] weight, and, in fact, it has an almost exact counterpart (in dimensions and weight) at Chanhu-daro', notes Shereen Ratnagar in her study of the Indus–Mesopotamia trade.[7] She concludes that the weight probably indicates the presence of an Indus merchant trading at Ur. The first report of an Indus seal from Mesopotamia appeared just ahead of Marshall's 1924 announcement of the Indus civilization. In 1923 a mysterious seal carved with a bull motif and a three-character inscription was found at Tell Ahaimir, part of ancient Kish. Even earlier, shortly before the First World War, the Musée du Louvre in Paris acquired a well-preserved clay impression of a seal with a similar motif and a six-character inscription from a dealer who said the seal came from an unexcavated site in southern Mesopotamia, now identified as Umma. The impression appears to have originally sealed a jar, because the back of it carries 'a clean imprint of a cloth tied over a jar mouth by a string around the neck of the vessel', notes Tosi.[8] Its true significance emerged only after Marshall's announcement. In 1931, the year of publication of his *Mohenjo-daro*, the Louvre donated the seal impression to the Ashmolean Museum in Oxford, in view of its relevance to ongoing British research in the Indus valley.

On the other hand, there is not nearly so much incontrovertible evidence for the Indus–Mesopotamia trade as archaeologists might wish. Nissen refers to a 'meagre archaeological record'.[9] There is only one Indus weight from Ur, for example, out of a total of just fourteen Indus weights found in Mesopotamia, neighbouring Iran (Susa) and the Persian Gulf area. Only some twenty Indus seals have turned up in Mesopotamia since the earliest discoveries, of which nine have been dated to the Akkadian period (2334–2154 BC) and two to the Isin and Larsa dynasties (2000–1800 BC). In addition, from the islands of Failaka and Bahrain in the Persian Gulf have come more than one hundred 'Gulf-type' round stamp seals, many of them with a bison motif and an Indus inscription on the obverse and an Indus-style boss on the reverse, dated 2100–2000 BC. Almost certainly, the Persian Gulf – and Dilmun (Bahrain) in particular – was a vital commercial entrepôt.

The evidence is also complex, because some of the finds contain elements not found in the Indus civilization, which must have arisen from adaptation to local Mesopotamian conditions. For instance, some of the carnelian beads found in Mesopotamia are engraved with cuneiform inscriptions, whereas carnelian beads from the Indus area never carry an Indus inscription. (Two such engraved beads are dedicated by the Akkadian king Shulgi to the goddess Ningal as booty from his war against Susa.) And later, 'Dilmun-type' stamp seals, modelled on the above-mentioned 'Gulf-type' stamp seals, carry a motif influenced by Mesopotamian, rather than Indus, glyptics, without any inscription. Looked at overall, the Indus–Mesopotamian seals were 'probably a product of some place under the influence of both the Indus and the Sumerian civilisations', noted the Assyriologist C. J. Gadd as early as 1932.[10]

Other cuneiform inscriptions offer ambiguous clues. Assuming that the name 'Meluhha' in cuneiform does refer to the Indus civilization, as is widely agreed, it is clear that the Indus area was a source of Mesopotamian luxuries. A well-known Sumerian myth, the story of Enki and Ninhursag, refers to Meluhha as a source of carnelian. An inscription of Gudea, the king of Lagash in 2144–2124 BC, mentions carnelian, gold dust and other Meluhhan luxuries used in the construction of Gudea's main temple in Lagash. According to Parpola, such luxuries may have included water buffaloes, presented as royal gifts to Sargon. This king received ships from Meluhha at his capital Akkad, as mentioned earlier. There is no textual indication that the ships carried water buffaloes. However, comments Parpola, the water buffalo is depicted in the Indus seals, yet never depicted in Mesopotamian art – until after the start of the trade with the Indus area. At this time, during Sargon's lengthy reign around 2300 BC, the buffalo suddenly replaced the wild aurochs bull in the vital 'contest' scene of Mesopotamian art, in which a warrior (presumably the king) is shown spearing a wild beast to prove his strength. If Parpola's theory is correct, the ships from the Indus valley must have been roomy enough and sturdy enough to transport large animals.

Did merchants and artisans from the Indus area settle in Mesopotamia? Here again the evidence is inadequate for certainty, but distinctly implies that they did. In the first place, the adaptation of Indus styles to local taste was surely done by Indus craftsman working on the spot. The faceted version of drilled carnelian beads and the pear-shaped version of a decorated carnelian bead were both styles unique to Mesopotamia, presumably created by local demand. 'These clues suggest that merchants or entrepreneurs from the Indus valley may have set up shops in cities such as Ur to market their goods and also produce objects in local designs', writes Kenoyer.[11] The excavator of Ur, Leonard Woolley, took the same view in his book *Ur 'of the Chaldees'*: 'By the time of the Akkadian dynasty, if not before, trade between Sumer and the Indus valley had attained such proportions that there may have been agents from that distant region in Mesopotamia.'[12]

Textual evidence supports this interpretation. Multiple cuneiform texts dating from towards the end of the third millennium BC refer to a village in southern Mesopotamia, close to Lagash, by the name Meluhha. Either this was the name of the village or the name of some people residing there – probably the latter, because the village is also called Guabba. Of these people, 4,272 were women and 1,800 were children, all of whom worked in Lagash as weavers. Maybe Meluhha village was a colony of expatriate Indus weavers, who settled in the area when the direct Mesopotamian trade with the Indus civilization began to fade away. More convincing, perhaps, is an Akkadian cylinder seal from the time of Sargon. This shows a seated person of high rank, royal or divine, receiving two standing visitors. A bearded dwarf perches on the seated person's lap, his head turned to face the dignitary. The first visitor seems to be addressing the seated dignitary with the help of a hand gesture, as is the dwarf. The seal's accompanying cuneiform inscription reads as follows: '*su-i-li-su / eme-bal me-luh-ha*', which translates as: 'Su-ilisu, interpreter of the Meluhhan language' – possibly the name of the dwarf (opinions differ). Sadly, no more is known about Su-ilisu. 'We can imagine that, like the other Meluhhans, he had established some close ties within Mesopotamia', speculates Wright. Perhaps he began as a merchant from the Indus area, learned how to speak Akkadian and then 'forged a new profession as a translator' for his fellow merchants.[13] Alternatively, he could have been an Akkadian-speaking native who saw a business opportunity through learning the language of Meluhha. Either way, this unique seal offers some slight encouragement that Mesopotamian excavation may one day yield the Holy Grail of Indus script decipherment: a bilingual inscription written in both cuneiform and the Indus script.

If the chances of finding such an inscription in Mesopotamia are small, the chances of finding it in the Indus area are vanishingly small. Evidence for the Indus–Mesopotamia trade may be limited in Mesopotamia, as we have seen; but in the Indus valley it is virtually nil. According to Kenoyer, 'no items produced in Mesopotamia proper have been found in the Indus region.'[14] According to Parpola, 'the only object of clearly western Asiatic origin in the Greater Indus Valley is a "Dilmun-type" seal from Lothal', the port town that certainly traded with Dilmun (Bahrain).[15] Other scholars are slightly more indulgent. Ratnagar claims that a handful of bar-

Indus–Mesopotamian interaction. This impression (top right) of an Akkadian cylinder seal (top left) from the time of Sargon (2334–2279 BC), with drawing (bottom), carries the cuneiform inscription: 'Su-ilisu, interpreter of the Meluhhan language'. Meluhha was the Akkadian name for the Indus valley.

rel-shaped weights found at Harappa, Mohenjo-daro, Dholavira and Lothal must have been made in Mesopotamia, since they resemble Mesopotamian weights. But such a physical resemblance is far from conclusive proof of their origin, as Marshall, who discovered Mohenjo-daro's barrel-shaped weights, cautiously noted: 'This type of weight was used in Egypt . . . It is found in considerable numbers in Mesopotamia . . . Weights of this shape were also common in early times in Elam.'[16] The cubic weight found at Ur almost exactly matches one found at Chanhu-daro, whereas the barrel-shaped weights from Indus sites do not exactly match similar weights from Mesopotamia.

If traders and artisans from Mesopotamia personally lived and worked in the Indus cities – as Indus traders seem to have done in Mesopotamian cities (and maybe the village of Guabba) – then Indus archaeologists would definitely have expected to find some cuneiform accounting tablets, cylinder seals and seal impressions of the kind that are so plentiful in Mesopotamia itself. However, there is no trace of cuneiform in the Indus cities, and only a few cylinder seals, none of which resembles Mesopotamian seals in style or execution; they may have belonged to Indus traders dealing with Mesopotamia, rather than Mesopotamian traders personally working in the Indus valley. This absence of evidence is, of course, what we should expect if the Mesopotamian traders sailed only so far as the Persian Gulf, not to the Indus area itself.

To justify and sustain this international trade, what was in it for the Indus traders? What kind of Mesopotamian products did they need and desire? Whatever these were, the imports must have been perishable, and hence invisible to archaeologists. It seems unlikely they included much food, since the Indus dwellers already had plenty of grain and other foodstuffs, though we might imagine the Indus area importing dates from the Persian Gulf (Oman), as South Asia does today. Metals and semi-precious stones seem unlikely imports, too, given the existing sources in the Indus area of most metals and stones like carnelian and lapis lazuli, though again we might postulate the import of silver from Mesopotamia, and perhaps pearls from the Gulf. Textiles, and especially wool, are likely candidates for importation, however. The Indus people apparently did not produce wool, as mentioned earlier, whereas the Mesopotamians produced woollen textiles on an industrial scale, which were probably regarded as the finest available. Another likely candidate is incense. Incense burning is first recorded in ancient Egypt, occurred in Mesopotamia and seems to have been important in the Indus civilization, judging from an unidentified object frequently depicted on the seals next to the unicorn motif that appears to have been an incense burner. Both wool and incense are mentioned as exports in Mesopotamian cuneiform texts.

Plainly, this account of the Indus–Mesopotamia trade is not fully satisfactory. Trade and trade networks were without doubt highly developed in the Indus area from an early period, and they surely played a key role in knitting together the Indus cities, towns and villages into a civilization. And yet, what should have been the single biggest sector of this trade – that with Mesopotamia – seems to have been highly skewed in favour of Mesopotamia. There exists 'a gaping hole in the middle of this picture', as McIntosh remarks, since there is 'apparently almost nothing that the Indus people were getting from their trade with Mesopotamia and little from the rest of the Gulf'.[17] With so low an apparent economic return to the Indus area, and no direct contact with the area by Mesopotamians (leave alone their colonization of the Indus valley), it is difficult to see how the trade with Mesopotamia could have played a key role either in the formation of the Indus civilization in the mid-third millennium BC or, for that matter, in the demise of the civilization in the early second millennium. Sumerian civilization almost certainly influenced the art, society and religion of the Indus; but it seems highly unlikely that Mesopotamia's material wealth provided the stimulus for the Mature period in Harappa, Mohenjo-daro and other Indus cities.

SEVEN

SOCIETY

T
he connection between the Indus area and ancient Mesopotamia in the economic sphere, however obscure the trade in the opposite direction may have been, was paralleled by an extraordinary *dis*connection in the political and social spheres. The Indus polity and Indus society look totally unlike their contemporary equivalents in Mesopotamia. The starkness of the difference is evoked in Woolley's famous account of excavating the Sumerian royal cemetery at Ur, which included some objects from the Indus valley, such as carnelian beads and an inscribed seal. This occurred during the late 1920s, in the very same years when Marshall was excavating the Great Bath and other buildings at Mohenjo-daro.

Here Woolley describes the drama that his digging exposed in one of Ur's royal 'death-pits':

> The pit measured, at the bottom, 27 feet by 24, and had the usual sloped approach and its sides had been mud-plastered and hung with matting. Six men servants carrying knives or axes lay near the entrance, lined up against the wall; in front of them stood a great copper basin, and by it were the bodies of four women harpists, one with her hands still on the strings of her instrument. Over the rest of the pit's area there lay in ordered rows the bodies of 64 ladies of the court. All of them wore some sort of ceremonial dress; a few threads and patches preserved by being in contact with stone or metal showed that this had included a short-sleeved coat of scarlet, the cuffs

enriched with beadwork in lapis lazuli, carnelian, and gold, with sometimes a belt of white shell rings; it may have been fastened in front with a long pin of silver or copper; round the neck was worn a 'dog-collar' of lapis lazuli and gold together with other looser necklaces of gold, silver, lapis lazuli, and carnelian beads; in the ears were very large crescent-shaped ear-rings of gold or silver and twisted spirals of gold or silver wire kept in order the curls above the ears. The head-dress was much like that of Queen Puabi; a long ribbon of gold or silver was looped several times round the hair and, at any rate with those of higher rank, a triple band of gold, lapis lazuli, and carnelian beads was fastened below the ribbon with gold beech-leaf pendants hanging across the forehead. 28 of these court ladies wore golden hair-ribbons, the rest silver . . . It must have been a very gaily dressed crowd that assembled in the open mat-lined pit for the royal obsequies, a blaze of colour with the crimson coats, the silver, and the gold; clearly these people were not wretched slaves killed as oxen might be killed, but persons held in honour, wearing their robes of office, and coming, one hopes, voluntarily to a rite which would in their belief be but a passing from one world to another, from the service of a god on earth to that of the same god in another sphere.[1]

No burial even remotely resembling this lavish Sumerian burial has turned up in excavations in the Indus area. Indus burials, which are relatively rare, contain the very simplest of ornaments, such as a shell bangle, no weapons and no hint of human sacrifice, whether of menservants or courtiers. None is dedicated to a royal figure or a great leader, so far as can be seen from the context. Nor do they show any signs of violence. Whereas ancient Mesopotamia in the third millennium BC was a land of powerful and boastful kings like Sargon and Shulgi, of warfare between city-states like Akkad and Susa, of palaces and great temples such as the Great Ziggurat of Ur, the Indus civilization apparently managed without kings, courts, military arms, palaces or public temples of any kind. Perhaps these are referred to in the characters of the undeciphered script, as they are in the cuneiform seals and tablets –

but looking at the design of the Indus seals, this seems unlikely to be the case.

The political and social organization of the Indus civilization is, frankly, still something of a mystery. This situation has led to a great deal of informed guesswork by scholars, who sometimes radically disagree. The original excavators at Harappa and Mohenjo-daro tended to see the uniformity of these cities – which was in many ways so striking – as evidence for a unified state, governed by some kind of corporate structure rather than a single ruler of the kind indubitably present in Mesopotamia and Egypt. Their view continued to dominate the field of Indus archaeology, even as archaeologists uncovered more and more settlements in the 1950s and after. Thus Parpola, who has worked in the field since the 1960s, is confident that 'The Indus leaders had a strong authority that undoubtedly had an ideological foundation. Priests played a vital role in the administration.'[2] And Possehl, equally long serving, imagines (in admittedly speculative vein) that:

> the Indus peoples were ruled by a series of 'councils' or gatherings of leaders, rather than a king . . . There may have been civic councils for individual settlements, regional councils for the Domains or the political unit above the civic, and possibly a supreme 'Indus Council'. I sense in the Indus peoples a marked distrust in government, per se, especially strong, centralised government.[3]

Not every expert is persuaded of a guiding authority and ideology, however. Nine decades of Indus archaeology have demonstrated not only the uniformity of the civilization, but also its diversity. Chakrabarti acknowledges the prominence of 'common cultural elements' between sites – most obviously the Indus seals and script, and the weights and measures – but declines to see these elements as indicative of political unity. 'Instead of visualizing a civilization based on an empire divided into different zones, each with a metropolis' – for example, Mohenjo-daro in Sindh, Harappa in the Punjab and Dholavira in Gujarat – 'we should adjust to the view that there were many smaller kingdoms, city-states or other kinds of independent polities.'[4] Wright goes somewhat further than Chakrabarti, stating that: 'The lack of uniformity in the Indus [civilization] argues against a strictly shared conception of religious or administrative buildings or an overarching authority common to all cities.'[5]

Let us see what evidence there is for a central authority that succeeded in imposing itself over the Indus area. The prevalence of peace over a long period is usually taken to be one sign of such an authority. Peace seems to have prevailed over the Indus area in the second half of the third millennium BC. Was it imposed by force? It appears not. Apart from the generally agreed absence of military weapons in excavations, Indus art scarcely depicts fighting. Bows and arrows made of cane are depicted, but the only definite scene of fighting in the entire corpus of Indus art is a cylinder seal from Kalibangan. It shows two men apparently fighting over a woman in a long skirt with long braided hair and bangles on each hand. Each man grabs one of her hands, while their spears form an arch over her head. They are watched by what looks like a female deity with the body of a tiger and the horns of a markhor goat. So the scene is partly mythical. Even if it also represented fighting between mortals, notes Kenoyer, 'Both men are dressed in the same manner, suggesting they are from the same ethnic group, so it is clearly not a battle to protect a woman from an outside raider.'[6]

In the real world, it is at least arguable that the Indus people would have had no need to take up arms against outsiders because

Impression of a cylinder seal from Kalibangan showing two men apparently fighting over a woman. Violent scenes are extremely uncommon in Indus art.

'they lacked a natural enemy', as McIntosh speculates with considerable persuasiveness.[7] They had plenty of land, food and raw materials, so they had no incentive to invade foreign lands. Who might have attacked them? To the west, their relations with the people of Baluchistan were good, judging from the settlements at Mehrgarh and Sutkagen-dor, and the same probably applied to Afghanistan to the north and northwest, on the basis of the Indus settlement at Shortugai; to the east, in Rajasthan, there was desert and the Aravalli ranges with a low population density. Only in the south, along the coast, might the Indus dwellers possibly have faced armed attack from the sea, including by pirates. But here they enjoyed considerable seafaring prowess and could have defended themselves. However, 'It may be in this context that the strongly fortified towns of the coastal regions should be viewed', claims McIntosh, echoing Wheeler.[8] As for Mesopotamia, Indus relations with it were commercially excellent; it was relatively distant from the Indus area, separated by mountains; and anyway, the city-states of Mesopotamia were preoccupied with their own wars against immediately neighbouring lands.

Further evidence for a central Indus authority comes from the anti-flood platforms underlying various Indus cities. Earlier we noted that the vast scale of organized effort required to build the platform at Mohenjo-daro must have been motivated by the destruction caused by the annual floods of the Indus. This is a reasonable assumption. To carry out the gigantic task, one presumes that the labour force, though voluntary, would have required mobilization, direction and provisioning by a central authority, in the absence of slavery, for which there is no evidence. The construction of the pyramids at Giza in ancient Egypt at around the same time as the foundation of Mohenjo-daro in the mid-third millennium BC would appear to be an apt comparison, since the former is thought to have been accomplished by a strong ruler but without the use of slave labour.

The existence of successful trading networks over a vast area in and around the Indus valley is also suggestive of a central authority. It is difficult to see how such networks could have developed and operated effectively for five or six centuries without an infrastructure of basic roads between settlements, presumably maintained by taxation, and also some kind of regulatory framework to enforce the validity of a commercial agreement made by a trader at, say, Lothal, when he was subsequently trading at distant Harappa or even more distant Shortugai. Both the maintenance of roads and the framing of regulations would have required an urban-based coordinating authority with responsibility for numerous settlements, not just one city. Indeed, a good case can be made that trade, and the specialized technologies on which much Indus trade depended, might have legitimized such a coordinating authority in the eyes of the average Indus dweller. For the cities, through their workshops, controlled the production from raw materials of objects such as shell and stoneware bangles, carnelian beads and gold jewellery, which were used to define social status and conduct rituals. Furthermore, the area-wide system of standardized weights lends credence to the idea of a central authority. These weights clearly worked well, because the system survived long after the disappearance of the Indus civilization.

Most telling of all in this context are the seals, since they are found in every part of the Indus area (as well as in the Persian Gulf and Mesopotamia). They must originally have been conceived by a central authority and backed by its prestige – rather like the ubiquitous coinage of modern nations, which is backed by the reputation of a central bank. But rather than acting as a currency, the Indus seals were almost certainly markers of identity. Exactly how this identity was defined by the seal motif and accompanying inscription is of course unknown. Leaving aside the inscriptions for later analysis, what may plausibly be said about the motifs? Kenoyer offers one interesting interpretation:

Square stamp seals with animal motifs carried messages understandable to all the different communities living in the Indus cities. As a totemic symbol, the animal represented a specific clan or official, and additional traits, such as power, cunning, agility, strength, etc., may have been associated with each animal. At least ten clans or communities are represented by these totemic animals: unicorn, humped bull, elephant, rhinoceros, water buffalo, short-horned humpless bull, goat, antelope, crocodile and hare. Of these, the unicorn may represent the most numerous and widespread clan, and because of the sheer numbers of unicorn seals it is unlikely that they all represent rulers. The name or title of the owner was carved along the top of the seal.[9]

Other scholars are less enamoured of the clan idea. Some suggest that a particular animal might have been associated with a particular city, for example, the unicorn motif with Mohenjo-daro, where the unicorn is the commonest motif among the city's seal finds. Alternatively, an animal might have been associated with one of a small number of key occupational groups, such as farmers, potters, metalworkers or priests, who would presumably have existed in all settlements. In theory, analysis of the frequency and location of discovery of particular seal motifs within a settlement, and comparison of this data across settlements, might help to distinguish the most likely explanation for the motifs. In practice, however, too many unknown or uncontrollable factors disrupt such an analysis: the fact that seals were sometimes accidentally dropped and lost when their bosses broke; the unavoidable incompleteness of excavations at many sites, including Harappa and Mohenjo-daro; and the assumed tendency of seal-owners to move their residence. For instance, the unicorn motif is common at Harappa (46 per cent of seals), if not quite as common as at Mohenjo-daro (60 per cent). Does this fact falsify the idea of the unicorn's supposed association with Mohenjo-daro, or could it be that many seal-owners from Mohenjo-daro settled in Harappa over a long period, yet retained their original, Mohenjo-daro related, unicorn seal motif while living and working in their adopted city? In such a way surnames have spread in the modern world, from particular parts of the countryside to cities and even to other countries, as individuals have migrated and emigrated to find work and new ways of life.

If there was a central authority but no king, how did Indus society establish a social hierarchy? Clans based on ties of blood are naturally a possibility. So are occupational groupings. The strong evidence for diverse specialization in sophisticated crafts, and the apparent emphasis on bathing, has led a few scholars to postulate that Indus society was held together by a caste system comparable with the later Hindu caste system. The latter is based on birth, occupation and a concept of ritual pollution, with Brahmin priests forming the highest and purest caste. McIntosh even postulates that the very first Brahmins, mentioned in the Vedic literature, may have been 'descendants of the former native ruling class' of the Indus civilization.[10] A significant problem with all such speculation is that Hindu caste involves more than simply social class, craft and career specialization and an aristocracy of relatively austere Brahmins; it depends on an underlying philosophy of a cosmic order, expressed in the concept *rita* in the Rigveda, the text in which the first indisputable hint of the concept of caste appears, which foreshadows the later, better-known Hindu concept of *dharma*, the eternal law of the cosmos. Since the Indus inscriptions cannot be read, nothing definite can be said about Indus philosophy, and whether it had a comparable idea of caste.

Instead of looking fruitlessly for the existence, or not, of an invisible Indus caste concept, some hints of an Indus elite and social hierarchy may emerge from a study of burial practices, the use of ornaments and perhaps sculptural details – despite assuredly limited evidence. Inhumations and cemeteries have been discovered at only five sites in the Indus valley: Derawar, Harappa, Kalibangan, Lothal and Rupar – none at Mohenjo-daro (despite the discovery there of unburied bodies, as mentioned earlier). Mostly, these burials contain carefully laid-out skeletons. There is only very occasional evidence for cremation (the typical method of disposal of the dead in later Hindu society), such as the human ashes found at Harappa by Madho Sarup Vats in just one out of 230 urns. In fact, 'the only unequivocal evidence for cremation at an Indus site', writes Possehl, comes from at least five cremations found on top of an artificial platform at Tarkhanwala Dera, 90 kilometres from Kalibangan.[11] It is also possible that the dead were deposited in water, or exposed so as to allow excarnation by animals.

Overall, there is no sign in the bones of the skeletons that some individuals were better nourished than others: everyone, not just

Grave of an adult male at Harappa. He was interred wearing a long necklace of 340 graduated steatite beads, three separate pendant beads made of natural stone and three gold beads.

an elite, seems to have enjoyed access to a sufficient and balanced diet. Nor is there much display of personal wealth in the graves (in utter contrast to the graves of Mesopotamia and Egypt), assuming that the burials have not been disturbed by robbery, for which there is no evidence in the Indus area. As a grave offering, there may be some simple pottery, but no high-value items, such as copper tools, gold jewellery or long carnelian beads, and no seals (which suggests that seals were not personal possessions). The skeleton itself often wears modest personal ornaments such as a necklace or bangle, which is usually a shell bangle; no terracotta, faience, copper or stoneware bangles appear in graves. Intriguingly, the shell bangles in the earliest graves at Harappa (dated about 2600 BC) are slightly less wide than those found in the latest graves (dated about 2000 BC), which may indicate that the women who wore them – perhaps members of a social elite – became less involved in heavy manual labour over many generations. In general, there seems to have been no strong belief in an afterlife, for which the dead person needed to be provisioned, but instead a practical attitude to material wealth. As Kenoyer observes:

Precious metals, gold and valuable stone beads were generally kept in circulation among the living, while only the most essential personal objects were buried with the dead: shell bangles, beads with eye designs, steatite disc beads and mirrors. As a whole, the burial customs further reinforce the importance of ornaments and public symbols to define social and ritual status among the living.[12]

The small number of surviving Indus sculptures may or may not depict an elite, with the obvious exception of the 'dancing girl'. Are they portraits of real individuals or images of deities, or perhaps deified portraits? There is really no way of knowing; and so scholars are divided. Kenoyer first concludes that the sculptures are not 'images of rulers', on the reasonable grounds that there is no tradition of royal portrait sculpture in classical India.[13] (Not even the emperor Asoka was portrayed.) But subsequently he contradicts himself by stating that the sculptures are likely to have depicted 'influential citizens or even rulers at Mohenjo-daro'.[14]

The so-called 'priest-king' sculpture of Mohenjo-daro lacks even the slightest evidence that it is a portrait of a real person. It may be a deified portrait of a particular priest, but even this limited identification is based on aesthetic and cultural arguments, as mentioned earlier, since there is no firm evidence for temples or priests in the Indus civilization. Nonetheless, there is no denying the aesthetic power of the iconic little steatite statuette. As Chakrabarti sardonically observes, its singular presence has been used by scholars to 'justify an entire priesthood'.[15] There is also no denying the evidence for what looks very much like religion in Indus society. But whether this religion was a unifying influence resembling Hinduism in Indian society, as has often been claimed since the time of Marshall, turns out to be controversial.

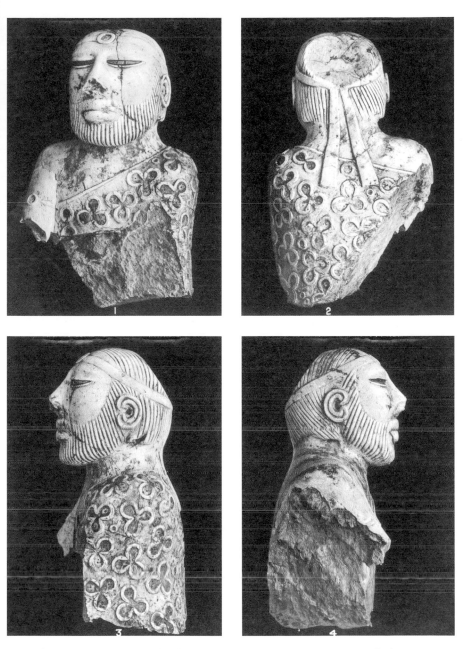

'Priest-king' statuette made of steatite, from Mohenjo-daro. It is 17.5 cm high, 11 cm wide.

EIGHT
RELIGION

In any ancient society, religion is notoriously tricky to reconstruct without having access to scriptures. Think of the
tantalizing European Palaeolithic cave paintings of animals
and human hunters at Lascaux and Altamira, where no writing
exists. What sense could scholars make of the convoluted myths
in the Egyptian Book of the Dead, simply by looking at tomb
paintings without reading their hieroglyphic texts? Or of the
imagery from the ancient Mesopotamian myths, such as the epic
of Gilgamesh, without reading Sumerian cuneiform tablets?

In the Indian subcontinent, the Vedic period does not suffer
from this handicap, because of its extensive literature, that is,
the Vedas, the Upanishads and other early Hindu scriptures,
composed orally between about 1500 and 500 BC and in due
course written down in Sanskrit. On the other hand, the Vedic
period signally lacks any archaeological remains; the only significant ones from the period are some city walls at Rajagriha in Bihar
dating from the early to mid-first millennium BC. The Indus civilization, by contrast, certainly lacks any scriptures, since its script
(which may or may not contain religious thought) is undeciphered.
Yet it offers extensive architectural remains. But which of the Indus
remains can be shown to be religious? Was the Great Bath at
Mohenjo-daro essentially a religious building, rather than an elaborate swimming bath? Were the city's numerous, small, stone objects
– roughly cylindrical in basic form, in some cases shaped into a
tip – phalluses comparable with the much later Shiva *lingam* of
Hinduism, rather than, perhaps, game pieces? Marshall was

inclined to answer both of these questions in the affirmative during the 1920s. Today, some scholars agree with him, while others are more inclined to caution, especially about the purpose of the stone objects.

Even Marshall, however, openly confessed there were no recognizable Indus temples, to his considerable surprise and disappointment given the obvious constructional skills of the Indus builders. In *Mohenjo-daro*, he writes:

> no building that can definitely be stated to have been a temple has yet been found either at Mohenjo-daro or Harappa. This does not by any means prove that no temples were built. Many buildings have been found that are clearly not ordinary dwelling places or administrative buildings . . . though at present we cannot determine their uses with any degree of certainty, and the objects found in them, unfortunately, prove nothing. Indeed, for all we know, the temples of Mohenjo-daro may, for conservative reasons, have been of wood and perished altogether. Whatever their form and material, one thing is certain, viz., that they did not in anyway resemble the temples of Sumer or Babylonia. No trace of a ziggurat with its associated temple has been unearthed at either Mohenjo-daro or Harappa . . . Up to date not a single building has been found whose plan in any way resembles that of the Babylonian temple with its temple-tower, its large open court for worshippers well supplied with water, and its especial shrine for the god or goddess at the end of the court. This alone would, in my opinion, suffice to show that the religions of the Sumerians and the Indus Valley peoples were dissimilar.[1]

Despite almost a century of subsequent excavation, no self-evidently religious structures have been found at any Indus site to contradict Marshall's account. The only exception might be the sacrificial hearths dubbed 'fire altars', discovered at several Indus sites, including Kalibangan, Lothal, Nageswar, Rakhigarhi and Vagad. At Kalibangan these consist of clay-lined pits containing ash, charcoal, the remains of a clay stele and terracotta cakes; at Lothal, a terracotta ladle with smoke marks was found near such a hearth. However, not every expert is convinced they are sacrificial hearths: at Nageswar, 'the "fire altar" is in all likelihood a regular Indus funnel-shaped updraft kiln', according to Possehl.[2] The most convincing examples – from Kalibangan – recall the Hindu ritual of libation of the five products of the cow (milk, sour milk, clarified butter, urine and dung) in the presence of a fire as offerings to a clay *lingam* in the worship of Shiva. There is a parallel, too, with the Vedic fire ritual, which involves the libation of milk at sunrise and sunset. In this, the heated milk is considered to be the sun or the sun's seed poured into the womb: 'Surya [the sun] and Agni [the fire] were in the same receptacle [*yoni*, "womb"]. Thereupon Surya rose upwards. He lost his seed. Agni received it . . . he transferred it to the cow. It (became) this milk.'[3] But while there is no doubt that sacrifice at fire altars was integral to the Vedic religion, there is no proof that the excavated Indus hearths – if that is what they really are – constitute fire altars in the Vedic sense. 'The similarities have been overemphasised and the shared elements of fire and animal sacrifice are too common, being found in many religions, to be a culturally diagnostic link', notes McIntosh.[4]

In the absence of scriptures and temples, speculation about the Indus religion must rely on imagery: in figurines and sculptures such as the 'priest-king', and on pottery and seals, many of which show mythical scenes. It begins with the very early ceramic female figurines from Mehrgarh. What was their purpose? Was it religious, or were the figurines merely toys? The excavators found them frequently in rubbish deposits, where they seemed to have been haphazardly discarded, encouraging the view that they were toys. But more careful study by Catherine Jarrige has revealed that the rubbish deposits in question were often within the household area, which suggests the possibility that the figurines had a cultic significance. Some of them also contain small holes running through the figurine, probably created by small twigs when the clay was soft, which add to the impression of cultic significance (as in the device of sticking pins in a voodoo doll). Moreover, the fertility attributes of the figurines, such as their bulbous breasts,

'Fire altars' at Kalibangan. These clay-lined pits containing ash, charcoal and terracotta objects may have been sacrificial hearths.

broad hips, prominent hairstyles and even a child in the arms, are combined 'so systematically that they must conform to certain rules with definite symbolic connotations', comments Jarrige. 'With good reason, therefore, we can discount the suggestion sometimes made that these figurines are in fact children's toys.'[5]

But it is the seals that naturally invite the most attention and prompt the most ingenuity in interpretation. Not only do they depict composite fantasy animals – some with three heads – as well as real ones, they also depict interactions between animals, humans and what can only be deities. Let us take a closer look at three particularly promising seals. The first shows a godlike human figure surrounded by animals, excavated by Mackay and quickly dubbed 'a prototype of the historic Shiva' by Marshall.[6] The second

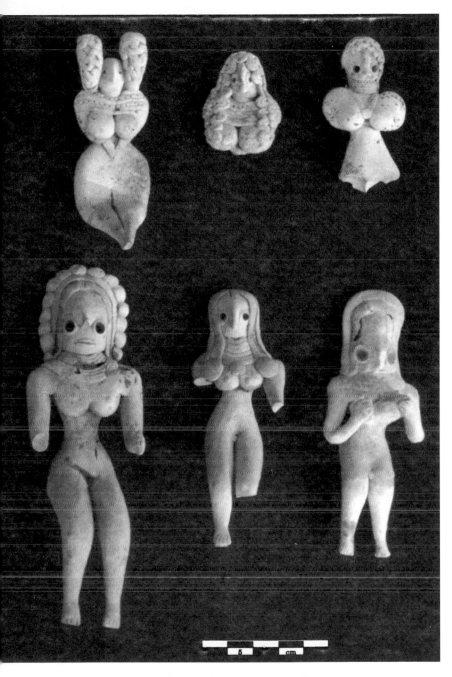

Female ceramic figurines from Mehrgarh. The earliest figurines date from 7000 BC.

concerns a mysterious object that generally accompanies the unicorn motif. The third is a highly complex scene of worship, apparently of a goddess in a peepal tree, which may involve human sacrifice.

Marshall's 'proto-Shiva', which may well be the most celebrated of all Indus seals, is a male figure seated upright in a clearly yogic posture, with his legs folded under his body and his feet pointing downwards (the posture known as *mulabandhasana*) on what appears to be a throne. He has three faces, one looking straight ahead, the other two looking sideways, to the left and right. His head is crowned with a spectacular three-pointed headdress including two curved buffalo horns. On his arms there are bangles. He appears to be ithyphallic. Arranged about him are four vividly depicted wild beasts, two on either side: a rhinoceros with a water buffalo and an elephant with a tiger. Above his headdress are characters from the Indus script.

Why did Marshall feel licensed to connect this Indus figure from the third millennium BC with the chronologically much later figure of the Hindu god Shiva, known only from the first millennium BC, who is never mentioned by name in the intervening Rigveda? Four attributes suggested this interpretation. First, the three faces of the figure fitted with the fact that Shiva is frequently three-faced (*trimukha*), a trinity, although Marshall qualified this argument by writing:

> I do not mean by this that the philosophic idea of a triad associated with the doctrine of the absolute had taken shape at this early period, but simply that the cult of this particular god – call him Shiva or by whatever name we like – had been amalgamated with [two] other cults, and that the fact was signified by giving him three faces instead of one.[7]

Second, the yogic posture fitted with Shiva's reputation as Mahayogi, the prince of yogis. Third, Shiva is also known as Pashupati, the lord of the animals – symbolized here by the rhinoceros, water buffalo, elephant and tiger. Fourth, a headdress with horns was commonly used to denote a deity, and also worn by priests and kings, in

Indus seal impression from Mohenjo-daro, with drawing, showing a three- or four-faced figure wearing a horned headdress and seated in a yogic posture, surrounded by four wild beasts. John Marshall, who discovered the seal, dubbed the figure 'proto-Shiva'; but solid evidence for this Hindu attribution is lacking.

ancient Mesopotamia; and more speculatively, this particular three-pointed headdress resembles in shape the famous trident (*trisula*) carried by Shiva. Finally, though this is not an attribute, the connection fitted Marshall's belief that the roots of Hinduism – in this instance, the god Shiva – lay not only in the Vedic culture of the Aryans but also in the pre-Vedic Indus civilization.

None of these arguments is entirely convincing; indeed, 'the evidence for any kind of continuity between this prehistoric god and Shiva is rather weak', according to the historian A. L. Basham.[8] Many scholars have come up with significant criticisms. For example, it makes more sense to imagine the deity as having four faces (one of them looking backwards, and therefore hidden), with each face matching one of the four animals. This would associate him with the Hindu god Brahma, successor of the Vedic creator-god Prajapati, rather than with Shiva. His erect phallus is not clear; this detail may instead be part of a knot in his waistband (as Marshall himself recognized). His yogic posture, which occurs in various other Indus seals, seems to have a non-Indian antecedent in the proto-Elamite art of neighbouring Iran dating from the early third millennium BC. The four animals that surround him are wild animals, with the possible exception of the water buffalo; yet the Hindu god Shiva did not protect wild animals. And since the horns he wears are buffalo horns, he should probably be associated with the Hindu buffalo demon, Mahishasura (*mahisha* is the Sanskrit for 'buffalo'), rather than with Shiva, who is usually associated with the bull (Nandi), though it is true that Mahishasura is sometimes identified with Shiva. How very much one wishes that the accompanying characters, which may well contain the deity's name, could be reliably read.

Consider now the second example of possible religious imagery, the 'unicorn'. When an animal motif, rather than a deity, is the focus of an Indus seal, it is sometimes depicted on its own, as is usual with the elephant, rhinoceros and tiger – perhaps because these are wild animals. But often it is shown with a specific object in front of the animal. In some cases, such as the short-horned and humpless bulls and the water buffalo, the object is almost always a feeding trough, which would have been filled with offerings of grain or water; similar types of shallow basin with downturned rims have been found in excavations. However, the unicorn motif is never depicted with the feeding trough, only with an unfamiliar object that has not been recovered from excavations. Most scholars believe this object had a ritual purpose, and it is difficult to disagree, despite much uncertainty about the nature of the ritual.

Kenoyer describes the object as follows:

> The ritual offering stand is made up of three parts, a tapering shaft or column which stands on the ground and pierces a hemispherical bowl-shaped container that is sometimes held on the shaft by a small pin. Projecting above the bowl, the shaft supports a square- or dome-shaped object. This top component is usually cross hatched with a grid or zigzag lines, and the bowl portion is variously depicted with cross hatching or horizontal lines. The edges of the bowl often have tiny dots or radiating lines along the bottom edge and sometimes even along the top edge.[9]

To Marshall, the object was an incense burner. The incense was placed in the upper container, which may have revolved around the shaft, while the bowl contained a fire, with its flames indicated by the dots or radiating lines along its top edge. Iravatham Mahadevan, however, identifies the object quite differently. To him, it is a filter for preparing a sacred, intoxicating drink, *soma*, that played a crucial role in later Vedic rituals. (The botanical identity of the plant used to make *soma* has been much debated but is now widely accepted as belonging to the genus *Ephedra*, the source of the drug ephedrine, a banned substance among modern sportspersons.) In this second interpretation, the upper container was a filter through which the liquid *soma* dripped into the lower bowl, with its overflow indicated by the dots and radiating lines on the bottom edge.

Our third example of religion in the seals includes an animal motif, a puzzling object, a deity and a worshipper, as well as other figures. This fascinating 'narrative' seal from Mohenjo-daro has been the subject of much speculation and is far from being fully understood. The deity stands inside a sacred peepal tree (*Ficus religiosa*), a fig tree divided into two main branches with their characteristic heart-shaped leaves – the same species as the Bo tree (or Bodhi tree) under which the Buddha achieved enlightenment and which today commonly provides shade over the tombs of Muslim saints in Pakistan. The figure wears a long braid at the back, numerous bangles on its arms and a horned headdress, so it most likely depicts a goddess, since tree deities in India (*yakshis*) are usually female. In front of the deity the suppliant, also wearing a horned headdress, kneels, and behind the suppliant stands a giant, human-faced markhor goat with a beady eye and two long curly horns, above which float several characters from the script. Beneath this scene, along the bottom of the seal, stands a procession of seven human attendants of the deity, all with long braids at the back, bangles and single-plumed headdresses, who are sometimes referred to as seven priestesses, although there is no definite evidence that they are female.

But the most intriguing detail is yet to come. 'What the small object is near the feet of the suppliant is uncertain, as the seal is slightly damaged at this point; possibly it is an offering to the deity on a small altar, or possibly an incense table', comments Marshall.[10] This seems reasonable, and as far as one may go in identifying the object. However, Parpola and some other scholars, including Kenoyer, boldly go further. To them, the object is probably a severed human head; indeed Parpola, after studying two curious protrusions from the object, maintains that it is a man's head with a double bun at the back typical of a male hairstyle seen elsewhere in Indus art and sculpture (as on page 129). If so, this 'fig-deity' seal would provide the only known example of human sacrifice in the Indus civilization – unless we propose the same interpretation for some seated male figurines with their legs together and hands clasped at the knees. 'This type of figurine has been interpreted as a worshipper,' writes Kenoyer, 'but perhaps it represents a sacrificial victim with hands and feet tied together.'[11]

In looking, however briefly, at Indus religion, it has been hard to resist drawing comparisons with Hinduism – whether with the god Shiva, Vedic rituals or tree deities. Another interesting example is the swastika motif. This ancient symbol, the name of which

'Fig deity' seal made of steatite, from Mohenjo-daro: one of the most intriguing Indus seal stones. This impression, with drawing, shows the deity on the right, a kneeling worshipper, a goat and seven human attendants. Some scholars identify it as a scene of human sacrifice.

signifies 'well-being' in Sanskrit, pre-dates the Indus civilization and occurs frequently in Indus seals and inscriptions – both in its left-facing and right-facing (Nazi) variant, sometimes even side by side on the same tablet. Its Indus meaning is unknown: possibly the two variants stood for different cults or philosophical schools. Certainly in later Hinduism and Buddhism the variants represented the opposing forces of the universe. Today in the Indian subcontinent, the swastika is very widely used both in Hindu religious rituals and secular life as a decorative symbol supposed to bring wealth and good fortune, for example on public buildings, domestic dwellings and the human body. Further intriguing examples of such continuities between the Indus civilization and present-day Hindu South Asia will appear in the penultimate chapter on the origins of Hinduism.

Having said this, we must remain mindful of the lack of solid evidence for Indus religion. No Indus temples, priests or rituals can be identified for sure. Moreover, there is little consistency in the conceivably 'religious' structures at different sites, by contrast with the consistency in other kinds of structure such as brick sizes, flood platforms and 'citadels', as well as the consistency in ornaments such as beads and bangles. To draw yet another comparison with later Indian religion, enormous diversity exists within Hindu beliefs, practices and rituals, not to mention the tribal religions that have influenced, and been influenced by, Hinduism. For example, human sacrifice has been practised in India, among certain Hindu devotees and certain tribes, at various times, though never as a dominant tradition. If Indus religion really is one of the roots of Hinduism, then it, too, may well have been remarkably diverse.

On the present limited evidence, it is surely possible there may have been *less* religion in the Indus civilization than the later Indian civilization might suggest, or than some scholars – beginning with Marshall – might wish. In the absence of a decipherment of the script, religious explanations have conveniently filled some yawning gaps in scholarly understanding. But is this wise? To my mind, the current Indus situation is uncomfortably reminiscent of the situation in ancient Mayan studies before the decipherment of the Mayan script in the 1980s and 1990s. According to the leading Mayanist of the 1970s, Eric Thompson, the ancient Maya rulers of Central America were a theocracy with a deeply spiritual outlook. Their ideal was 'moderation in all things', their motto 'live and let live' and their character had 'an emphasis on discipline, cooperation, patience, and consideration for others'.[12] Theirs was

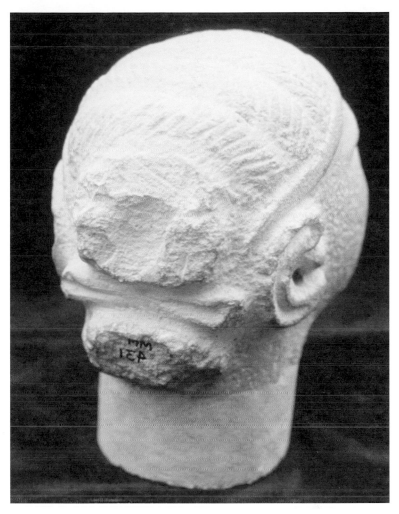

Male head from Mohenjo-daro, probably broken from a seated sculpture, showing combed hair tied into a double bun at the back.

a civilization unlike any other, said Thompson, who looked to the Maya as a source of spiritual values in a modern world that placed far more importance on material prosperity. Only thanks to the Mayan decipherment did Mayanists come to know that Thompson had been utterly wrong. The real Maya relished internecine war and the extended torture of captives; and both the Mayan rulers and their gods liked to take hallucinogens and inebriating enemas using special syringes. I am far from suggesting that the same volte-face will one day occur in Indus studies, if and when the script is deciphered. For now, though, it may be wise to assume that the Indus civilization was not a civilization unlike any other civilization – not least in the circumstances of its perplexing decline and disappearance.

NINE

DECLINE AND
DISAPPEARANCE

In trying to explain the decline and fall of civilizations, it seems
that humans have a deep-seated need to assume they are caused
by human agency, which generally translates into a story of
internal degeneracy falling prey to external invasion, as with the
decline and fall of the Roman empire under the onslaught of bar-
barian outsiders. In the case of the Indus civilization, archaeologists
– especially Wheeler and his colleagues – for some decades assumed
that an armed invasion of the Indus area by fierce nomadic Aryans
from the northwest was the chief culprit in its fall. Only in the 1970s
was this explanation seriously questioned as a consequence of the
new radiocarbon dates for the decline of the Indus cities, reinvesti-
gation of the supposed archaeological evidence for an invasion,
and convincing textual arguments disproving an attack on the
Indus cities derived from nuanced study of the Rigveda without
prejudice. Today, the idea of a concentrated Aryan invasion of
the Indus civilization has been wholly rejected by scholars, although
not the more flexible concept of a series of Indo-Aryan-speaking
migrations into the Indus area from Central Asia.

Likelier is some kind of environmental explanation. Destructive
climate change has been largely ruled out, as mentioned in the
introductory chapter. But natural hazards are surely a possibility.
They could have included changes in the Indus river and its tributaries triggered by Himalayan tectonic activity. These could have
caused the disappearance of the Saraswati river and, perhaps,
prolonged flooding of the Indus and salination of the fields used
for crops, as has happened in modern Pakistan, especially around

Mohenjo-daro. If so, river-borne trade – and also the ocean-going trade with Mesopotamia – would have declined. Moreover, water-related diseases such as malaria and cholera would have spread. Even a major earthquake should be considered, given some evidence of damage at two ancient Indus sites and the turbulent seismic record of modern Gujarat. However, there is no compelling evidence for an environmental force acting alone to destroy the Indus civilization.

Most probable is that the decline was the outcome of a combination of human and environmental factors. Furthermore, it was probably not catastrophic but actually quite gradual, given the striking variation in prosperity observed at different Indus sites during the centuries after the end of the Mature period around 1900 BC. Hydrological changes, floods and diseases might have played a part. So might deforestation caused by brickmaking and copper smelting. So, too, might an increasing rejection of central authority, possibly due to migrations of foreigners from the northwest. In addition, perhaps we should consider some inherent cultural weakness, related to the general uniformity of the civilization and its apparent absence of a military authority. 'The Indus ideology ultimately had feet of clay', claims Possehl in provocative mode. 'In the end their ideology made the Indus peoples who they were, but it may have proved to be their undoing as well.'[1]

Let us first look at the evidence for decline, then assess what evidence exists for both environmental and human factors, and finally see if this discussion suggests any definite overall explanation of the decline.

In the most recent levels of Harappa and Mohenjo-daro the early excavators found distinct signs of deterioration in the conditions of houses, drainage and urban existence. At Mohenjo-daro, huts were poorly constructed out of used and often broken bricks; kilns were built in the middle of streets; and some bodies were left unburied – which Wheeler famously took to be victims of a 'massacre' by invaders. Moreover, painted pottery largely gave way to plain wares and inscribed seals were no longer in use. The excavators concluded that these cities had been abandoned, and that this was also true in other parts of the Indus area. But excavations at many sites since the 1950s, including further excavation at

Unburied human skeletons lying haphazardly in a lane in the upper levels of
Mohenjo-daro date from the city's period of decline, *c.* 1800 BC.

Harappa, have shown this picture of universal abandonment to
be fictitious. A decline in the major cities undoubtedly occurred,
yet even in the cities it was not sudden or uniform: Harappa was
inhabited until about 1300 BC; and outside the urban centres there
is some evidence for an increase in economic activity. By Kenoyer's
reckoning:

> It took over one thousand years for the political and cultural
> centre of the northern subcontinent to shift from the Indus
> valley to the middle Ganga [Ganges] region. Because the process
> of change was gradual, it is unlikely that anyone living during
> the period between the decline of the Indus cities (1900 to 1300
> BC) and the rise of the Early Historic cities (800 to 300 BC) would
> have been aware of the shift.[2]

For example, in one particular area of Harappa, recent excavators found intact walls, hearths, charred grain deposits and ceramic vessels, some with inscriptions, which date from about 1700 BC, according to a radiocarbon date from a hearth. A new form of kiln dates from this period, demonstrating a development, rather than a regression, in technology. There was also a cache of typical Indus ornaments and objects, made from copper alloy, agate, carnelian and faience, including 133 beads. One of the beads was made of brown glass, the earliest known sample of glass from South Asia.

Some plant remains discovered in 1978 at Pirak, a second-millennium BC agricultural settlement close to Mehrgarh in the upper Kachi plain of eastern Baluchistan, 'provided an insight into the kind of rural landscape that emerged from the "ashes" of the Indus civilisation', argues Tosi. 'Far from being the catastrophic scenario historians had imagined from a literal reading of the Vedic epics, the image was now one of economic affluence and diversification', a century after the decline of urban life in the Indus valley. None of the earlier crafts was abandoned: Pirak's residents continued to work copper and lapis lazuli and obtain shell from the coasts. But new crops – rice and millet – supplemented the earlier barley and wheat. This mixed-crop cultivation probably supported the introduction of pack animals – camels and horses – and transformed the economic basis of the rural economy. 'By 1500 BC, Pirak presents us with a picture of the Indian village as it will become known to the first Europeans', writes Tosi.[3]

In the southern regions of the Indus – Kutch and Gujarat – the picture is decidedly mixed. At some sites there was a clear breakdown of settlement followed by an abandonment of the site, at others a continuity of settlement based on transformation. Thus at Dholavira, the eastern gate and other walled enclosures were subject to makeshift repairs, followed by the construction of circular houses not at all in consonance with the layout of the city and its architecture, which seem to suggest a breakdown in civic control. Lothal, too, was poorly repaired and then abandoned. So was Kuntasi, where its industrial complex was abandoned around 1900 BC and new houses were built of stone rubble; by 1700 BC Kuntasi was nothing more than a small rural village. Yet at Rojdi, in Saurashtra, the settlement flourished from around 1900 BC. In the words of its excavator, Possehl:

> Just as Mohenjo-daro was being abandoned, Rojdi was expanding in size. New houses and other structures were constructed on the fill of the South Extension; the Main Mound was rebuilt. The Large Square Building was constructed on the North Slope. The circumvallation, with a major gateway, was constructed around the landward side of the settlement, enclosing the South Extension and Large Square Building, as well as space between it and the Main Mound. This took the size of Rojdi from 2.5 to 7.5 hectares.[4]

In one crucial respect, no variation from site to site has been found. At the end of the Mature period, inscribed Indus seals disappear (the latest, from Daimabad in Maharashtra, dates from about 1800 BC) and give way 'to seals bearing nothing but geometrical motifs such as the swastika', remarks Parpola.[5] There are no seals from the Harappa excavation dating to 1700 BC, for example. On the other hand, the Indus script seems to have continued in use for a while, if only as a form of decoration, judging from recognizable Indus characters on pottery in the form of graffiti. Then it totally disappears. From the mid-second millennium BC until the third century BC (the beginning of the Asokan Brahmi and Kharosthi inscriptions) – in other words, for almost 1,500 years – there is no evidence for an indigenous writing system in the Indian subcontinent. Here is an extraordinary fact at first sight, given that this very period encompassed the composition of the Vedic literature and the rise of a caste of men who prided themselves on their worship of words. 'The disappearance of writing at the end of the Indus tradition in the north can possibly be correlated to an increase in the dominance of the Vedic ritual elites, Brahmins', notes Kenoyer.[6] The explanation for the disappearance has to be that these Brahmins revered the power of memory, rather than writing, because it enabled them to restrict the knowledge of the Vedic scriptures to their own caste. Their sacred literature was entirely oral and was written down only much later in the Hindu tradition.

Even today, Brahmin priests take pride in reciting the scriptures from memory rather than reading from manuscript sources.

Turning to the environmental factors behind decline, perhaps the most likely is a change in the course of the Indus, its tributaries and neighbouring rivers over a period of time, even centuries. This would inevitably have affected the water supply of certain cities, their flood risk and the flood risk to their surrounding areas. But before tangling with this tricky issue, it is well to consider the view of Dales, the last excavator of Mohenjo-daro (in 1964–5), who noted in the mid-1980s:

> No one disagrees that major flooding was part of the accepted routine of living in the central valley. It is the extent to which such flooding might have fatally disrupted the economy and contributed to the decline of the urban phase of the culture that is the problem. This involves a fascinating and complex multi-disciplinary type of research that is now beginning to receive serious attention from scientists.[7]

Dales recommended that archaeologists familiar with particular sites should collaborate with natural and physical scientists

River flooding in the Indus valley, 2010: a reminder that the Indus civilization was shaped by the changing course of the Indus river. Such changes may have contributed to the civilization's decline.

familiar with, for example, geology and hydrology. Some research along these lines was subsequently conducted. For the lower Indus region, a reconstruction of the Indus river's course based on historical sources, ground observations of geomorphic processes, landform reconstructions and aerial photography was published in 1993 by Louis Flam. It shows a considerable change in the course of the Indus during the period 4000–2000 BC, whereas the course of the Nara river, flowing to the east of the Indus in Sindh, remained the same in this period. Mohenjo-daro, lying strategically between the Indus and the Nara, may gradually have found itself 'in a hazardous position close to the brunt of the annual flood', concludes Flam.[8] Thick layers of silt in Mohenjo-daro bear witness to catastrophic floods. Flam suggests that flooding of the city caused by the long-term displacement of the Indus may have caused the eventual abandonment of the city.

Considerably clearer in its impact is the drying up and disappearance of the Saraswati river from the early second millennium BC. This may have been the downstream outcome of tectonic changes near the sources of the Indus in the Siwalik region of the outer Himalayas, which have long been uplifting the mountain range and altering the courses of rivers before they descend to the plains. By about 1000 BC the Saraswati had vanished, or alternatively, in a picturesque image from the Vedic literature, the blessed river now flowed underground to join the confluence of the Ganges and Yamuna rivers at Allahabad. Today, the Saraswati's ancient course exists partially as the Ghaggar-Hakra river system (the Ghaggar in India and the Hakra in Pakistan; see chapter Two), which flows only in the monsoon. Its gradual desiccation must have removed the water supply of the numerous middle Indus sites clustered along the Saraswati's banks, such as Ganweriwala, and forced their inhabitants to abandon the settlements. It must also have adversely affected sites on the lower Indus, by reducing the flow of the Nara river, the southern extension of the Ghaggar-Hakra river.

That said, 'The dwindling of the Saraswati took place over a number of centuries', writes McIntosh, 'and is unlikely to be the only reason for the Indus collapse.'[9] Another contributing factor may have been the ill-health of the population. The skeletons from the upper levels of Mohenjo-daro died not from violent attack, according to studies of their bones made by the forensic anthropologist Kenneth A. R. Kennedy published in the 1980s, but in many cases from malaria and probably other diseases. Malaria could have become more prevalent with flooding and cholera, which cannot be detected in such ancient bones, or it could have spread by contamination of drinking water, facilitated by the city's comprehensive drainage system if it had not been properly maintained, as seems to have been the case in the Late period.

Some evidence for earthquakes, which are notoriously difficult to establish beyond reasonable dispute at almost all archaeological sites throughout the early ancient world, comes from Kalibangan and Dholavira. At Kalibangan excavators detected displacement of deposits and subsidence of walls. At Dholavira they observed more unequivocal signs, suggesting an earthquake of major magnitude: slip faults in sections and the displacement of architectural features, which were subsequently repaired by the town's occupants. However, these observations pre-date the Mature period at Kalibangan and lie well within the Mature period at Dholavira, so they cannot be informative about the Late period. Nor is there any evidence for earthquakes around the end of the Mature period that might have contributed to a civilizational decline.

Nonetheless, the Kalibangan and Dholavira earthquakes indicate that earthquakes may have occurred fairly often during the Indus civilization. This would be consistent with seismic evidence from the historic period. Three major – if largely forgotten – earthquakes occurred in Kutch during less than 200 years, in 1819, 1956 and 2001. The first and last of these had an enduring impact on the region. Not only did the 1819 earthquake help to consolidate British rule in Kutch after 1815 by levelling walled towns hostile to the British, according to a contemporary colonial memoir, it also threw up a natural dam, known as the Allah Bund, which diverted the waters of the Indus and caused the fertile lands of Kutch to wither. 'As agricultural lands withered, the population of Kutch turned to trade, commerce and international migration for its fortune', writes the anthropologist Edward Simpson in his study of the effects of the 2001 earthquake. 'The earthquake produced

a new kind of people and society.'[10] For example, he argues, the
1819 earthquake was an important factor in generating the Gujarati
diaspora of the nineteenth century, which established the commercial reputation of Gujaratis overseas in today's world. As for
the 2001 earthquake, it destroyed a large part of rural and urban
Kutch, and its aftermath led to the resignation of the chief minister
of Gujarat. His hitherto-unknown successor as chief minister,
Narendra Modi, set about a radical industrial development of
Kutch. In 2014 Modi was elected prime minister of India, largely
on the strength of his economic record in Gujarat. Notwithstanding
the absence of archaeological evidence for earthquakes in the Indus
area during the early second millennium BC, they should not be
ruled out as possible factors in the political changes that must
have accompanied the end of the Indus civilization.

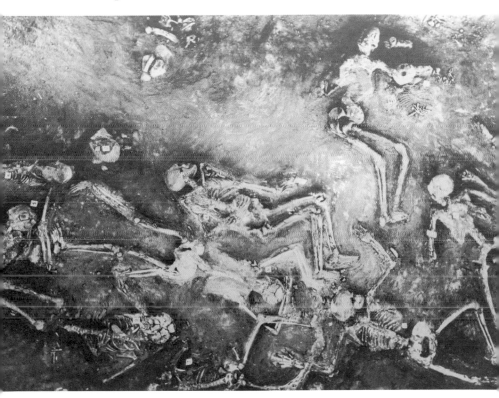

Victims of a massacre, or of disease? According to forensic study of these
skeletons at Mohenjo-daro, the people died from malaria and other diseases.

Leaving aside natural environmental factors, what about human ones? The burned bricks required to build the Indus cities must have required an enormous amount of fuel to feed the brick-making kilns, not to mention the fuel for the furnaces to smelt copper ore. Because no brick kilns have yet been discovered, as we already know, archaeologists cannot be absolutely sure what this fuel was. For decades they assumed that it was wood, which must have been obtained from felling huge areas of forest, on the basis that the climate of the ancient Indus valley was considerably wetter than today – thereby resulting in extensive deforestation and climate change. Today, however, both regional climate change and the existence of those ancient forests have been widely dismissed. Current studies suggest that there was adequate fuel for brickmaking in the scrubby natural vegetation of the Indus area, probably supplemented by the burning of cow dung.

A second human factor, the Indus trade with Mesopotamia, tailed off after about 2000 BC, though it probably did not cease for a century or two. However, the reason is not known. The trade could have declined because of political changes in Mesopotamia: the rise of the Babylonian empire under Hammurabi in the first half of the eighteenth century BC. This empire focused largely on trade with Anatolia and the Levant, and allowed the virtual collapse of the Persian Gulf trading network during the eighteenth century BC. Alternatively, the trade could have declined because of the abandonment of the Indus cities involved in organizing the trade. In other words, the decline in the Indus–Mesopotamia trade might have helped to cause the decline of the Indus civilization – or it may have been caused by it.

Lastly, there is the complex and vexed issue of migration into the Indus area from the northwest. The key to this now seems to lie in Central Asia, in an extensive and impressive culture discovered by Viktor Sarianidi in the 1970s in southern Turkmenistan and northern Afghanistan, areas then part of the Soviet Union. Now known as the Bactria and Margiana Archaeological Complex (BMAC), it lasted from 2400 to 1500 BC.

The BMAC must have interacted with the Indus civilization during the Mature period, perhaps via the Indus outpost at

Shortugai, because two Indus seals and some other Indus objects (ivory game pieces and dice) were found at a BMAC site, Altyn Depe, and a large Indus seal with an elephant motif and text at the BMAC capital, Gonur – both in Turkmenistan. But there is no evidence for any migration from the BMAC to the Indus area until the end of the Mature period. 'One might guess that the peoples of the BMAC sensed a vacuum in the Greater Indus region and moved in to fill it', writes Possehl.[11] According to Parpola, 'They brought to the Greater Indus Valley the domesticated horse, donkey, and camel and the Indo-Aryan language.'[12] He believes that an early wave of migrants came to Baluchistan (Sibri), Sindh (Chanhu-daro) and Rajasthan (Gilund) in about 1900 BC, followed by other waves in subsequent centuries, including the peoples who com-posed the Rigveda. In the course of the latter's migration, they subdued a hostile people, known in the Rigveda as the Dasas, who are said to have inhabited 99 fortified settlements. But whereas Wheeler assumed that the mysterious Dasas must correspond to the inhabitants of the Indus cities, the Vedic scholar Wilhelm Rau showed in 1976 that the Dasa forts had circular, and often multiple, concentric walls, totally unlike the walls of the Indus cities. Parpola proposes that the Dasas had no connection with the Indus cities: they were instead part of the earlier waves of migrants, who lived in fortified manors with concentric walls, which they inherited from the BMAC after about 1500 BC. This intriguing theory fits with both the description of the Dasa forts in the Rigveda and the shape of many forts excavated in Bronze Age Bactria and Margiana. But it is yet to be fully accepted. Even if correct, it leaves obscure the question of whether or not Indo-Aryan-speaking migrants played an active role in the decline of the Indus civilization.

Like the much better-documented collapse around 1200 BC of the Bronze Age civilization in the eastern Mediterranean (in-cluding the cultures based at Knossos, Mycenae, Troy and Ugarit and in New Kingdom Egypt), the disappearance of the Indus civilization remains puzzling. In the Mediterranean, it used to be thought that unknown 'Sea Peoples' were responsible. No one, however, has been able to identify them satisfactorily for the scholarly community, and so an invasion by the Sea Peoples no

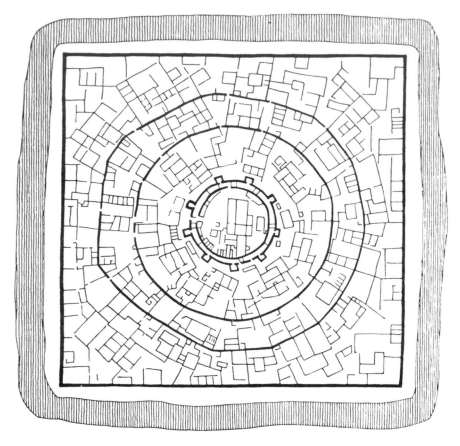

Ground plan of the 'temple-fort' at Dashly-3 in Bactria (north Afghanistan), with three concentric walls, *c.* 1900–1700 BC. Its design conforms to the forts of the Dasa people, as described in the Rigveda, and not to the cities of the Indus civilization.

longer washes as an explanation of the collapse of civilization in the eastern Mediterranean.

The latest scholar to consider the evidence, Eric Cline, concludes, a little lamely, that 'the end must have come as a consequence of a complex series of events that reverberated throughout the inter-connected kingdoms and empires of the Aegean and eastern Mediterranean.'[13] For the Indus area after 1900 BC the evidence is unfortunately infinitely less than is available for the eastern Mediterranean in 1200 BC. It appears that floods, diseases, earthquakes, trade disruptions, foreign immigration and perhaps a diminished central authority unsupported by military force are all in play. Those who like a story will probably want to believe, with McIntosh, that the Indo-Aryan-speaking migrations 'may not have caused the end of the Indus civilisation, but they sounded its death knell'.[14] My own hunch, for what it is worth, is that changes in the river systems of the Indus area accentuated existing weaknesses in the political structure of the Indus civilization and in due course undermined its unity and self-confidence. We are unlikely ever to learn the full truth. The best hope for further progress would seem to lie in a future decipherment of the Indus script.

TEN

DECIPHERING THE INDUS SCRIPT

The Indus script has been called, with irony, the most deciphered script in the world. The first claim to a decipherment, based on the Sumerian language, was published as early as 1925. More than a hundred published claims have been made since then, including the controversial example published in 2000 in *The Deciphered Indus Script* discussed in chapter One: that the Indus language is Vedic Sanskrit. But although there has been some definite progress in understanding the script over the decades, none of the 'decipherments' has persuaded anyone other than the proposer and a few others.

Even the number of texts is open to debate. Parpola counts about 5,000, Mahadevan 2,906 and Bryan Wells 3,835 inscribed objects. The total depends on how one assesses fragmentary and damaged inscriptions. The vast majority of the inscriptions – some 85 per cent, according to Mahadevan – were found at Harappa and Mohenjo-daro. About 60 per cent are on seals, but some 40 per cent of these are duplicate inscriptions, so the useful total for the would-be decipherer is not as large as it seems. More inscriptions were found in the 1990s, but the Indus script corpus is not abundant. Often, an inscription is tantalizingly brief: many consist of only a single character, the average has less than four characters in a line and five in a text, while the longest has only 26 characters divided among the three sides of a triangular terracotta prism.

In addition to the characters, many seal stones are of course engraved with an animal motif or an anthropomorphic figure (such as 'proto-Shiva'). How, or even whether, the animal motif relates to its accompanying inscription is totally unclear. A particular motif, such as the unicorn, may appear on many seals, each with a different inscription. Conversely, there are four instances of one and the same inscription occurring on two seals with different motifs. There are even two seals with the same inscription on either side but two different motifs.

The brevity of the inscriptions, and the dearth of both monumental inscriptions and temporary inscriptions (such as scribbles on potsherds) of the kind common in Mesopotamia, Egypt and elsewhere, have led a trio of scholars – historian Steve Farmer, computational linguist Richard Sproat and Indologist Michael Witzel – to doubt whether the Indus inscriptions belong to a writing system. In their view, the characters do not represent the sounds of a specific language: they are merely non-linguistic symbols, probably of religious significance. For a number of reasons, this theory seems unlikely to be true. Perhaps the most important are: that groups of characters recur in the same sequence at different sites; and that the characters can mostly be shown to have been written in only one direction (as we shall see). Sequential ordering and an agreed direction of writing are universal features of writing systems, as opposed to symbolic systems or artistic decoration, where such rules are not crucial. Moreover, the Indus civilization must have been keenly aware of the functioning of cuneiform writing in Mesopotamia through its trade links. On the other hand, the brevity might mean that the Indus characters belong to a partial writing system, capable of representing only limited aspects of the Indus language – rather than a full writing system such as Akkadian cuneiform and the English alphabet, that is, 'a system of graphic symbols that can be used to convey any and all thought' (as defined in 1989 by John DeFrancis in *Visible Speech: The Diverse Oneness of Writing Systems*).[1]

Assuming that the Indus script is a full writing system, several hopeful scholars have drawn a comparison with the recent Mayan decipherment. Like the Mayan script, the Indus script involves a large, complex and partly iconographic set of signs; and the names of neither places nor rulers are independently known (in contrast to the Egyptian hieroglyphs, where decipherers could turn to Greek and Roman historical sources). But there are clear-cut differences, as the Mayanist Michael Coe has pointed out. Mayan mathematics and calendrics were well understood long before the first linguistic breakthrough in 1952. Mayan inscriptions are 'numerous, often lengthy, and encode complete sentences', notes Coe. Modern Mayan languages are well known: 'The cultural context is rich and detailed, and many aspects of it survived the Spanish conquest.'[2] Lastly, and crucially, a bilingual is available (in the form of a Spanish-Mayan 'alphabet'). None of these advantages applies to the Indus script. Leaving aside the brevity of the Indus inscriptions, which may well contain mostly names and titles, scholars know virtually nothing of the calendrical system, are uncertain about the numerical signs, can make only informed conjectures about the language and culture, and lack anything resembling a bilingual. Above all, the Indus civilization disappeared more than 2,500 years before that of the Classic Maya, which is a long time, speaking either archaeologically or linguistically.

The vacuum of knowledge has been filled by serious scholarship as well as bizarre theories (some from reputable scholars) linking the Indus area with far-flung places. Both have been surveyed by Possehl[3] and separately by Parpola,[4] who notes:

> Connections have been sought with the manuscripts of the Lolos living in southern China and in Southeast Asia, dating back to the sixteenth century AD; with proto-Elamite accounting tablets; with ideograms carved some two centuries ago on Easter Island in the southeastern Pacific Ocean; with Etruscan pot marks ['More Seven League Boots!' comments Possehl]; with the numerical system of Primitive Indonesian; with Egyptian, Minoan and Hittite hieroglyphs; with the auspicious symbols carved on a 'footprint of the Buddha' in the Maldivian archipelago; and with the [Mayan] glyphs of ancient Central America.

Let us examine quite briefly four of the more serious claims, each by a respected scholar. Although they have been almost universally rejected, they have something worthwhile to teach us about how to tackle this difficult problem, and how not to. Note in what follows that all the inscriptions are read from right to left (we shall come to the evidence for this later).

The first of these 'decipherments', published in 1932, treated the Indus script as if it functioned like Egyptian hieroglyphs. Its author, the Egyptologist Flinders Petrie, did not postulate any connection between the Indus and Egyptian languages, but he did suggest that the pictographic quality of some Indus signs, their variants and their syntax might indicate their meanings on the Egyptian model, assuming that the seals belonged to officials and contained their titles. Thus Petrie read the Indus sign 𝕌, which is by far the most common sign, frequently found at the end of inscriptions, as a title meaning 'agent' ('wakil', in Petrie's terminology). The sign 𝕀 he took to be a tree with lopped branches, and the sign 𝕓 was said to be a writing tablet with a handle, a kind of hornbook. The sequence 𝕌𝕀𝕓 was therefore said to mean (reading from right to left) 'wakil [agent] of the registrar of timber'.

On a similar basis, judging that the Indus sign ▦ looked like the Egyptian hieroglyphic symbol for 'irrigated field', Petrie translated the sequence 𝕌▦ as 'wakil [agent] of irrigated land'. He also noted another very common sign and its apparent allographs (variants): 𝕏𝕏𝕏 𝕏𝕏. These signs are often found doubled: 𝕏𝕏 . Petrie decided that the first of the five allographs (on the far left) might indicate a title, inspector or intendant, while in combination the signs might indicate various grades of inspector, such as sub-inspector and deputy inspector – a 'most imaginative explanation' for the doubling, notes an amused Possehl.[5] To be fair to Petrie, he stressed that 'these are only suggestions, or speculations, and for "is" read "may possibly be" in all instances' – a sound caution, not often heeded by subsequent Indus script decipherers.[6] For even if Petrie were right, there would be no way to prove it, since his methodology was largely intuitive. But his suggestions did have one definite merit: they reminded everyone of the likely bureaucratic subject-matter of the inscriptions. That is, unless one takes the view, as some scholars have, that the Indus civilization is fundamentally different from Egypt, and indeed Mesopotamia, in its use of writing, and that the seals therefore probably contain esoteric ideas rather than economic matters.

The second 'decipherment', proposed by an Assyriologist, James Kinnier Wilson, linked the Indus civilization with the Sumerians. The two were said to have sprung from one stock, probably in India, and to have separated into two branches, with the smaller branch settling in Sumer and the larger in the Indus valley; thus according to the theory, the Sumerian and Indus languages were related to each other, which allowed their inscriptions to be compared.

Kinnier Wilson's approach, influenced by the clay tablets of Sumer, assumed that the Indus seals concerned economics: he called it 'the case for accountancy'.[7] The sign which Petrie read as 'inspector', ♙, Kinnier Wilson read straightforwardly as 'fish', and its variant ✕ he read, also pictographically, as 'carp', a freshwater fish common throughout Asia, which has thread-like filaments (known as barbels) hanging from its mouth. The Sumerian word for carp is *suhur*.

His next step was to equate Sumerian tablets from Uruk known to concern fish rations (below) with Indus 'fish' inscriptions from three different sources (opposite):

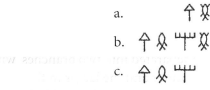

The key, for Kinnier Wilson, was that the Sumerian sign ⟨ba⟩, *ba*, meaning 'rations', looked like the final sign of the above Indus inscriptions. In the 1970s he had regarded it as a word-divider, but by the 1980s he changed his mind and allotted it (without other evidence) the meaning 'rations'. By further equating the Indus sign with a well-known Sumerian sign of similar shape, which means 'great' or 'large', he went on to offer the following interpretations of the above three Indus inscriptions:

a. carp rations (*suhur-ba*);
b. giant carp rations;
c. similar to b. – either this was an abbreviation, or the carp was sometimes known simply as the 'giant' fish, without 'carp' being specified pictographically.

The weaknesses in the 'Indo-Sumerian' approach are manifest. Why, for a start, does the 'fish' sign occur in b. with the 'carp' sign? Not the least of the flaws is the gross mismatch between the artistic excellence of Indus seals and the notion that many were intended as receipts for fish. But Kinnier Wilson's attempt, like Petrie's, also has one definite virtue: it reminds us of the risks of comparing sign shapes across cultures and our duty, if we do, not to manipulate the evidence to fit our preconceptions.

The third 'decipherment' came from the excavator of Lothal, Shikaripura Ranganatha Rao, an archaeologist who was at one time director of the Archaeological Survey of India. Rao proposed it in a large and detailed book published in 1982. It involved at least three radical assumptions. The first was that the Indus signs were mostly ligatures (compounds) of a smaller set of signs. Thus Rao analysed a series of signs as follows into ligatures of the common simple sign ⟨⟩ and other simple signs:

He concluded that there were 62 Indus signs – a figure far lower than that of the sign list proposed by almost all scholars.

By studying graffiti from Indus sites which appeared to post-date the Mature period of the Indus script (that is, to belong to the centuries after its disappearance around 1900 BC), Rao postulated the eventual development of an even smaller set of signs, about twenty in all.

Indeed, he assumed that the Indus script became alphabetic, and in doing so originated the alphabet, which was then transmitted to Palestine in the mid-second millennium BC, though Rao does not say how: his second assumption. (The consensus view is that the alphabet was invented in Palestine, based on the uniconsonantal signs of the neighbouring Egyptian hieroglyphic.)

This then enabled Rao to compare the signs used in the earliest Semitic alphabetic inscriptions with the 'Harappan' (Mature period) signs and the 'Late Harappan' signs on the graffiti.[8] Note that Semitic equivalents for the common Indus signs ☆ and ☆ are missing (opposite):

S. NO.	PHONETIC VALUE	OLD NORTH SEMITIC SIGNS 16th–13th c. B.C.	HARAPPAN SIGNS	LATE HARAPPAN SIGNS
1	b	⊏ 𝟗	□	□
2	g	∧ ↑	∧ ∧ ꓶ	∧
3	d	◌ △	◌ ◌	◌ ◖
4	h	⅃ ㅌ	ㅌ ㅌ E	⅃
5	w	Ɣ Y	Y	Y
6	ḥ	日 ⴺ	⊟ H H ⽥	⊟
7	th	θ ⊕	⊘ ⊙	⊘
8	ḳ	∨ ↓	↓ ↓	↓
9	n	5 5	∫ ∫	∫
10	s	≢	≢	≢
11	(ʿy)	○ ○	○	○
12	p	𝖩 ○ ◇	○ ◇) 〕	○ ◇
13	r	٩ ٩	ϸ	ϸ
14	sh	W W	W	W
15	t	+ X ⋏	X ⋏ ✕	⋏
16	ś	ᒧ •	ᒧ ↑	↑
17	ḫ	ꙍ •	ꙍ 8	
18	m	ꙅ •	K ɑ	K
19	a	ⴾ ⴾ ⴾ	U	U
20	ṛ		⚠	⚠
21	ś		⚘	⚘

Now – this is the third assumption – Rao applied the phonetic values of the Semitic letters to his Indus 'alphabet': which permitted him to read the Indus inscriptions. The words produced by his readings suggested to him that the Indus language was closely related to Vedic Sanskrit. He therefore derived the 'missing' phonetic values for the two common signs just mentioned from Vedic Sanskrit, not from the disobliging Semitic signs. The content of the inscriptions turned out to be names, titles and other epithets.

There is no independent archaeological, cultural or linguistic support for any of Rao's three assumptions – especially his belief that Semitic sound values are applicable to an Indo-European (Indo-Aryan) language, Sanskrit. It is hard to avoid the conclusion that Rao, for nationalistic reasons, was yet another Indian determined to prove that the Indus language was the ancestor of Sanskrit, which must therefore be an indigenous language, not an immigrant to the subcontinent.

The fourth, and final, 'decipherment' was the work of the excavator of Allahdino, Walter Fairservis, an archaeologist who spent decades digging in the Indus valley and surrounding areas (as well as in Egypt), partly sponsored by the American Museum of Natural History. In 1983 he published a long article on the Indus script in *Scientific American*, which became a book in 1992, in which there is no doubt that the author, like Rao, thinks he has 'cracked' the problem. (I recall the amused disbelief of a British Museum curator of Indus seals, who had just had them all 'read' for him by a visiting Fairservis.) However, Fairservis, unlike Rao, rejected early Sanskrit as the Indus language and favoured an early form of Dravidian, the family of languages currently spoken in south India.

Fairservis's method was both simple and complex. It was simple because it boiled down to three steps. First, decide what an Indus sign 'looked like' iconically or iconographically. Second, choose a word from a Dravidian language that fitted the chosen visual meaning. Third, determine the range of possible Indus meanings of the sign, arising from its definition in Dravidian, based on archaeological, cultural and linguistic evidence. The complexity, of course, came from the ambiguity introduced in each step. Signs resemble different things to different people (first step); there are usually several different words that fit any selected 'icon' (second step); finally, different scholars derive very different conclusions from the same pieces of evidence, especially when these pieces conflict (third step). And this is not to mention the important fact that, if the Indus language really is Dravidian, it must be a proto-Dravidian language some 2,000 years older than the oldest attested Dravidian words in the Old Tamil inscriptions of the state of Tamil Nadu in south India (probably third century BC). How reliable a guide to its earlier form is any language at so great a temporal remove?

Perhaps the best example of these difficulties is the sign ⚶ . Most scholars regard it as a 'fish', while differing as to its significance. But Fairservis preferred to see a twist, loop or part of a knot. Some of his reasons give pause for thought, such as the fact that the Indus scribes seem always to have drawn the sign with an under-over technique as one would a loop (but perhaps not a fish); the fact that many variants of the sign have small 'bodies' and enormous 'tails'; and the fact that all known Indus valley fishes have several fins, not just one pair. Following his intuition, Fairservis went on to identify various Dravidian words for 'twist', 'loop' and 'net', and settled on *piri*. This he now connected to another Dravidian word *pir*, meaning 'chief'. Hence he 'translated' the 'fish' sign and its variants (including the so-called 'carp' sign) as follows:

⚶ *pir* a chief of ordinary rank

⚶ *talpir* head chief

⚶ *acci-pir* elder

⚶ *maru-pir* chief priest

No one has agreed with this, for the very good reason that it is highly subjective (and Fairservis had no training as a linguist, certainly not in the Dravidian languages). Even Possehl, a devoted student of Fairservis, summing up his survey of all the many significant 'decipherments', felt compelled to write:

> Since there is little basic research on the script and so little sharing of programmatic visions, it is scarcely a wonder that the writing system has not yet been understood. With everyone reaching directly for The Grail, based on his or her own genius, it seems highly unlikely that the work could be used in a productive, additive program of research, since it is all so idiosyncratic. There is little reason to agree with Fairservis when he says: 'I believe that the [Indus] script is now well on its way to final decipherment because of these [i.e., his] efforts.' In fact, just the opposite seems to be the case.[9]

The comment about lack of basic research underestimates the fruitful labours of several distinguished researchers, especially Mahadevan and Parpola, as we shall now see. But the rest of the criticism, that each Indus script scholar strives to 'go it alone' – a criticism that cannot be levelled at the Mayan decipherment – has considerable point. But then, one might counter that the Indus script problem is so intractable that only someone with a high degree of confidence in his/her own intuition would think of trying to solve it.

Having scrutinized four over-optimistic 'decipherments', let us turn to some more cautious and logical approaches to the Indus script. How far is it possible to advance purely by internal analysis of the inscriptions, without taking a stab at guessing the Indus language? As we shall now see, one can settle the matter of the direction of writing and reading; establish an approximate number of signs and a sign list on which there is considerable agreement; agree on some of the numerals; and show that certain texts are likely to be segmentable into words.

To begin, it is necessary to establish that it was the seal impression that was intended to be read, not the seal itself, in which the characters are naturally reversed. (There is room for some doubt here, as seals far outnumber seal impressions, and many of the seals are hardly worn, suggesting that they were not used as stamps but perhaps as identity 'cards' or even amulets.) Fortunately, the correct orientation is easy to establish, because we can compare the sequences and orientations of characters in seal impressions with the same sequences in inscriptions that were clearly meant to be read directly, for example, pottery graffiti and those on metal implements. Generally, they match.

As for the direction of writing, we might expect to obtain a clue from the direction in which directed pictograms such as 🐚 face. In Egyptian hieroglyphic, for example, the pictograms face in the direction opposite to that in which the writing should be read. But it turns out that while the main image on the Indus seal impressions (such as the unicorn motif) generally, but not invariably, faces to the right, the direction in which the Indus script characters face is inconsistent.

The most dependable evidence for the direction of reading comes from the spacing of the inscriptions. If a short text starts from the right-hand edge and leaves a space on the left, it may be assumed to run from right to left. And if it shows cramping of characters on the left-hand edge, the same conclusion may be drawn. For instance, this seal impression:

In a second seal impression:

the sequence Ⲏↂ is found nowhere else in the inscriptions in the furthest left position, whereas ⴸⲎↂ is found there 76 times, as observed by Parpola. This suggests that the scribe was forced by lack of space to put the last character on the second line, and that the inscription should be read from right to left. (The alternative, left to right, would produce the pairing ⴸⴸ, which is found only *once* elsewhere, in the middle of an inscription.)

More striking still is the following seal impression from Harappa:

Plainly, the reader started at the top right-hand corner, turned the seal clockwise through 90 degrees twice, and part of the third edge and all of the fourth edge were blank.

Other decisive evidence regarding reading direction comes from another simple seal impression:

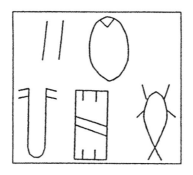

In the 1970s Mahadevan established from a detailed analysis of the corpus of inscriptions that " O is the most frequent pair combination in the Indus script. Out of 291 instances, the combination occurs 245 times at the right-hand end of a line. U is, as already mentioned, the most frequent Indus sign. Out of 1,395 occurrences, it is found at the left-hand end of lines 931 times. This must of course mean that there are some seals in which the above two orientations are not obeyed – but they are relatively uncommon. Statistically speaking, it is very unlikely that when the pair combination and the single sign appear together on one seal, as here, both will be written untypically (that is, that the pair combination will appear not at the right-hand end of a line and the single sign will appear not at the left-hand end of a line), so we can conclude that the normal direction of the Indus script is from right to left. However, there is a significant number of left-to-right examples of the script (6.6 per cent of the corpus, according to Mahadevan), and nine undeniable examples of boustrophedon (Greek for 'as the ox ploughs'), that is, writing in which alternate lines are written in opposite directions.

Some of the basic tools in successful decipherments have been a sharp photographic corpus with drawings (if the photographs are insufficient to see details), a reliable sign list and a concordance indexing the occurrence of each sign in the corpus. For the Indus script, these have been the work of Mahadevan and Parpola from the 1970s onwards, although they have worked separately, if amicably. Parpola's three volumes of photographs covering the collections in India, Pakistan and elsewhere revolutionized the study of the script, and his 1994 sign list, containing 386 signs with twelve more unnumbered signs (as against Mahadevan's 419 signs), are generally recognized as fine achievements, not least by Mahadevan, who notes that Parpola's sign list replaces all other sign lists, including his own. Allowing a margin for allographs and undiscovered signs, Mahadevan reckons that 'the present best estimate for the total number is 425 ± 25 signs.'[10]

This is an important figure. It is far too many signs for a syllabic writing system (or an alphabet, like that proposed by Rao), and far too few signs for a script like the Chinese characters, in which there are thousands of characters known as logographs ('word-signs'). The nearest comparisons might be Sumerian cuneiform with perhaps 600-plus signs, or Mayan glyphs with about 800 signs (though many of these are hardly used). Most scholars therefore agree that the Indus script is probably a *logosyllabic* script like its West Asian contemporary – although there has been little progress in identifying the signs for phonetic syllables.

Parpola has also, with his collaborators, standardized the signs and thereby computerized them to make a concordance, but this has met with somewhat less enthusiasm. Computerized analysis is a good idea in principle, but it is potentially misleading if based on a doubtful sign list. We certainly cannot rely on a computer to make judgements about which signs are allographs (variants) and which are ligatures (combinations of two or more simple signs). Rao, at one extreme, favours the reduction of the sign list to 62 signs, by ruthlessly eliminating allographs and ligatures, while at the other, Wells proposes almost 600 signs: a step that Parpola regards as retrograde. While no one (except Rao) has favoured such a drastic loss of potential information, it is much less clear where to draw the line at the higher end of the sign spectrum: in other words how many potential allographs and ligatures to distinguish as separate signs, so as to err on the side of disambiguation. In compiling an Indus sign list there is little to go on except the external forms of the signs, 'and any such procedure is bound to be arbitrary and subjective', admits Mahadevan.[11]

Nevertheless, a few techniques are available. We know that the signs Y and ↑ are allographs, because they are each found paired with more or less the same two dozen signs, and they occur inter-changeably in the common sequence ∪ Y ▭ : ∪ ↑ ▭. And we know from positional frequency analysis that the three signs ∪ ∪ ∪ are probably *not* allographs of the simple sign ∪. (The small strokes might, for example, be allographs, like the various accents on a vowel in French, é, è and ê.) For though this very frequent simple sign occurs often at the end of inscriptions (in the final position), as we know, it occurs only *once* out of 1,395 total occurrences at the beginning of inscriptions (in the initial position). The relevant figures for the other three signs are:

Ư 20 initial positions out of 177 total occurrences
Ữ 4 initial positions out of 35 total occurrences
Ữ 25 initial positions out of 51 total occurrences.

'It seems likely that Ư, Ữ and Ữ are indeed related to Ư, but that they are to be regarded as distinct signs, in a distinct functional subclass of their own, and not as mere allographs', writes Steven Bonta, who has attempted to analyse the Indus signs without making any assumptions about their language.[12] But as Parpola – who distinguishes four distinct signs in this particular case – notes: 'Application of the context criterion can be very convincing if the signs have a high frequency, but when they occur a few times only, the conclusion is bound to remain open to doubt.'[13]

Identifying the Indus numerals has proved a special challenge. Groups of short strokes of varying number (1–10 and 12, but not 11) occur in the inscriptions, for instance with the 'fish' sign that appears below in the uppermost left, as do groups of long strokes (1–7). Do these groups represent numerals, and if so, what is the difference between the short and the long strokes?

Complicating the situation is that there is frequent use of single and double short strokes in an obviously non-numerical way: the single short strokes often surround a sign like a sort of cartouche, and both single and double short strokes appear in the same texts as groups of long strokes. (The short strokes look as if they might be word-dividers, but other evidence we shall discuss in a moment suggests that they are not.) Of course, single and double short strokes could be capable of acting both numerically and non-numerically, depending on their context – compare the Roman numerals v, x, c, m, which are also letters of the Roman alphabet.

The occurrence of the group of 12 short strokes also seems inconsistent with its being a numeral. Therefore, ignoring the groups of 1, 2 and 12 short strokes, Mahadevan did a frequency count of the remaining groups of short strokes (3–9) and revealed the following numbers of occurrences in the corpus of inscriptions:

		Frequency
3	|||	151
4	||||	70
5	||| ||	38
6	||| |||	38
7	|||| |||	70
8	|||| ||||	7
9	||||| ||||	2

The abrupt drop in frequency after 7, and the fact that there are no groups of long strokes greater than 7, suggested to Fairservis that the Indus civilization counted in base eight (as opposed to our base ten) – a possibility enhanced by the fact that there is evidence for a Dravidian base-eight system. But this contradicts a considerable amount of other evidence that the Indus numerical system used base ten, with the following signs representing 10, 20, 30 and so on:

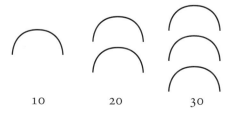

| 10 | 20 | 30 |

Perhaps, therefore, more than one system was used, for different purposes (for example, counting and weighing), as in the Indus weights. At least one researcher, Bonta, believes that the various 'fish' signs, which regularly occur with groups of short strokes, were actually used for counting; according to him they represented quantities in a measuring system.

The current uncertainty around the numerical system is well brought out in this comment by Parpola:

> Numbers seem to be represented by repeated long vertical strokes only in the early inscriptions (the miniature tablets of Harappa). In the Mature script, the smaller numbers (ones) are written exclusively with short strokes (in one or two tiers), while the long strokes have some other meaning. This can be concluded from the fact that the number of short strokes varies in front of specific pictograms (especially ⚸, Υ and U), while the number of long strokes does not (to any significant degree), except in the early texts. Moreover, the long strokes in the later inscriptions do not cover all the numbers represented by the short strokes, and they occur much less often, mainly in a few predictable sequences.[14]

Obviously – and everyone agrees about this – the numerical system needs much further study, of the kind brought to bear on Mesopotamian accounting tablets. However, since the Indus inscriptions are almost certainly not accounts, they are unlikely to yield straightforward answers to questions about counting. Both Mahadevan and Parpola have therefore retained separate sign numbers in their respective sign lists for the groups of long and short strokes.

Which brings us at last to the question of word-dividers and how the Indus texts may be segmented. One of the most convincing techniques involves choosing a long text and searching for its constituent sequences within the corpus. It is highly likely, for example, that there is a word boundary after the first two characters of this seven-character seal impression:

This is because we know of two other seal impressions which together make up the sequence in the above impression:

We may even postulate a second boundary within the seven-character text – perhaps a phrase rather than a word? – by examining a fourth seal impression that contains the final three characters of the above seven-character text:

At first sight, the single and double short strokes in some inscriptions, such as the seven-character inscription just considered, appear to be word-dividers. This is certainly a plausible interpretation of the double and single short strokes in the following two comparisons taken from five different inscriptions:

But the theory is challenged by inscriptions in which the double and single short strokes occur one after the other:

Also, they occur most frequently after the very first character of an inscription, an odd position for a word-divider; and at the end of inscriptions, where a word-divider is least needed. And, as Parpola remarks, 'If the sign I is really a word-divider, it is difficult to understand why the sign should be so frequent in a very limited number of contexts',[15] for example:

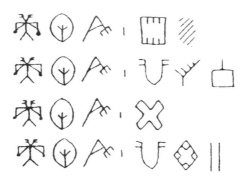

– rather than occurring regularly throughout the corpus, as would be expected of a word-divider.

A more reliable method of segmenting words is by the use of pairwise frequencies, that is, the total number of occurrences of a sign pair in the corpus. A high pairwise frequency indicates a high affinity between the two signs and hence that the pair may be part of a word, while a low frequency indicates a weak junction, probably a word boundary. Thus, in a six-character Indus text, ABCDEF, such as the following text segmented by Mahadevan, we may compare the frequencies of the adjacent pairs of signs AB (83), BC (17), CD (1), DE (40) and EF (93):

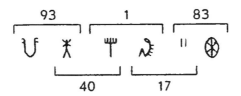

Word boundaries appear to correspond to the low pairwise frequencies 1 and 17, so we segment the text as follows (with the double short-stroke sign falling next to a word boundary but now not thought to be a word-divider):

$$\text{℧} \quad \text{⁂} \quad \text{Ψ} / \text{⩙} / \text{‖⊕}$$

'By this method almost all the long texts can be segmented into constituent phrases and words', writes Mahadevan.[16] There is, however, room for doubt in cases where the pairwise frequencies do not differ substantially.

Thus far, this chapter has presented a consensus view of the Indus script, with clear signposts towards minority opinions. From here on, it will be more speculative. But some speculation is better informed than other speculation. To avoid total confusion – an all-too-present risk in Indus script decipherment – we shall stick with ideas that are taken seriously by one or more respected scholars.

The overriding question is naturally the language of the script. Even to attempt an answer, one must first discount the possibility that the Indus language has completely died out. Discounting this has some rationale, given the exceptional cultural continuities of Indian civilization, such as the centrality of the Vedas in present day Hinduism. Then, one must examine the Rigveda, as the earliest surviving Indian literature, to see what it can reveal about the origins of the language families of the modern Indian subcontinent – Indo-Aryan (in the north), Dravidian (chiefly in the south but also in the centre), Munda (chiefly in the east) and Tibeto-Burman (on the fringes of the Himalayas) – plus one or two other languages, notably Burushaski, a language isolate from northernmost Pakistan, close to the Chinese border.

The Sanskrit of the Rigveda is, of course, an Indo-Aryan language. Yet, it has been shown to contain about 380 loan-words from the other Indian languages mentioned above, which must therefore have existed in Vedic times. The largest Vedic substratum is certainly Dravidian, which would seem to indicate a strong interaction between Indo-Aryan-speakers and Dravidian-speakers during the second millennium BC. Scholars have therefore argued

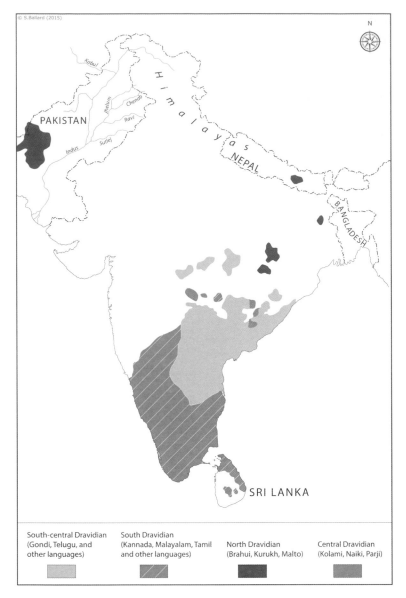

© S.Ballard (2015)

N

PAKISTAN

Kabul

Jhelum

Chenab

Ravi

Sutlej

Indus

Himalayas

NEPAL

BANGLADESH

SRI LANKA

South-central Dravidian (Gondi, Telugu, and other languages)	South Dravidian (Kannada, Malayalam, Tamil and other languages)	North Dravidian (Brahui, Kurukh, Malto)	Central Dravidian (Kolami, Naiki, Parji)

Map of the two chief language families of the Indian subcontinent, Indo-Aryan (white) and Dravidian (shaded), and the sub-divisions of the Dravidian family.

that the pre-Vedic language of the Indus civilization must be either Indo-Aryan or Dravidian, without entirely ruling out Munda, a possibility favoured by Witzel and another scholar.

The Indo-Aryan hypothesis is totally ruled out if one accepts that the Indo-Aryan languages arrived in the Indus area (from Central Asia) only after the Mature period of the Indus civilization. Moreover, the urban culture excavated at Harappa and Mohenjo-daro shows remarkably little resemblance to the pastoral society described in the Rigveda – an important point we shall investigate later. However, Hindu nationalists reject these chronological and comparative arguments, and insist that the language of the Indus script is similar to Vedic Sanskrit.

At first sight, the Dravidian hypothesis also seems improbable, given that today's Dravidian-speakers belong almost exclusively to south India, far away from the Indus area. Closer examination, however, shows pockets of Dravidian languages surviving in northern India, such as Kurukh, Malto and Brahui. The last of these is spoken by around 300,000 nomadic people in Baluchistan, which lies significantly close to the Indus valley. Brahui-speakers could be remnants of a Dravidian-speaking culture once widespread in the north that was submerged by encroaching Indo-Aryan-speakers in the second millennium BC: what Marshall termed 'an island of Dravidic speech which may well be a relic from pre-Aryan times'.[17] Conceivably, instead, the Brahui could have migrated to the northwest from south India, although it seems unlikely that a people would migrate from the relatively clement plains of India into the rugged mountains of Baluchistan. 'If the Brahuis were not the indigenous inhabitants of Baluchistan, who were?' asks Parpola reasonably enough. 'Certainly not the Baluch, who came from northern Iran in the tenth century AD or later.'[18]

The Dravidian hypothesis, unlike the Indo-Aryan hypothesis, is therefore plausible, if unproven. On the working assumption that it is correct, one can try to look for sensible links between the meanings of words in the early forms of Dravidian languages such as Tamil, Telugu, Malayalam and Kannada, and the iconic and iconographic signs and images on the Indus seals and other inscribed objects, taking help from both Dravidian culture and religion and from archaeological evidence about the Indus civilization. This is what scholars such as Fairservis, Mahadevan, Parpola and many others have done, sometimes with intriguing results. The problem is, no one can be sure if their interpretations are correct or fanciful.

The simplest example was first suggested in the 1950s by the Jesuit father Henry Heras (who lived in India), an influential figure despite some of his nonsensical suggestions. The word for fish in almost all Dravidian languages is *mīn*. In many Dravidian languages *mīn* also means 'star'. Could the very common 'fish' sign on the Indus seals have been pronounced *mīn* but have had the dual meaning 'fish' and 'star', which, as Parpola demonstrates, is an emblem of divinity and can thus stand for 'god'? The 'fish' sign could then be a rebus forming part of a theophoric name – a very common occurrence in Indian culture, where people are often named after gods and goddesses (for instance, Rama, Krishna, Ganesh, Indira, Lakshmi, Arundhati).

One could object to this: why is the star not represented pictorially too, like the fish? English-speakers are used to representing a star with a few short lines crossing at a point ('twinkling', so to speak), but this is just our particular convention, which happens to distinguish all the other stars from the Sun, which we generally represent with a small circle with 'rays' sticking out of it. It is quite conceivable that the Indus writers could have chosen a different and more subtle approach based on a homophony in their language between the Indus words for fish and star that English does not possess. (An English parallel might be 'son' and 'sun'.) As Robert Caldwell, the bishop of south India who identified the Dravidian language family in the 1850s, beautifully observed:

> Who that has seen the phosphorescence flashing from every movement of the fish in tropical seas or lagoons at night, can doubt the appropriateness of denoting the fish that dart and sparkle through the waters, as well as the stars that sparkle in the midnight sky, by one and the same word – viz., a word signifying that which glows or sparkles?[19]

Parpola has extended Heras's initial 'decipherment' and given an interpretation of a striking series of symbols on the seals, in which a 'fish' sign appears alongside a number of strokes that appear to be numbers. Parpola reads 'fish with three strokes' as *mum mīn*, Old Tamil for 'three stars', that is, the asterism (the small constellation) Mrigasirsa; 'fish with six strokes' as *aru mīn*, 'six stars', the Pleiades; and 'fish with seven strokes' as *elu mīn*, 'seven stars', Ursa Major.

Mahadevan comments cautiously:

> It is interesting to note that the numerical names for the three asterisms are actually attested in Old Tamil. There is however no proof that these interpretations are the only correct ones. There are, in the Indus texts, several sets of 'number + sign' sequences. The interpretation of 'number + fish' signs as asterisms would make this set unique among such sequences.[20]

Another of Parpola's several readings concerns the fairly common Indus sign depicting a pair of intersecting circles: ⊙. He identifies this as 'ear/nose rings' or 'bangles'. (Fairservis takes it to mean the number eight!) There are substantial numbers of fine stoneware bangles from the Indus excavations, as we know, many of them inscribed with script signs; and as Parpola points out, the 'intersecting circles' sign occurs in these bangle inscriptions with a frequency disproportionate to its occurrence in non-bangle inscriptions – suggesting that its meaning may be related to bangles. Other more complex and disputable evidence, based on the occurrence of ⊗ in various seal inscriptions, suggests that it might express the name of a deity. A Dravidian word for bangles is *muruku*, which is nearly homophonous with Murukan, the principal deity of the early Tamils, youthful god of war and love. Therefore, says Parpola, the sign showing intersecting circles may represent Murukan; and he supports this proposition with references to earrings and bangles in a variety of Indian religious and folk traditions.

Again Mahadevan, who feels that Parpola is over-inclined towards religious explanations of the Indus script, is attracted but sceptical:

> It is very likely that the interlocking circles do pictorially represent a pair of bangles. But when you try to give a phonetic value for it, this becomes very difficult. Parpola has chosen a word which means twisted wire bangle, or twisted wire amulet or a twisted wire earring or nose ring – where the operative word is twisting: the root is *murugu*, which means in Old Dravidian 'to twist'. But the polished vitrified stoneware bangles have no twists in them, so that is very unlikely. There are other words for bangles but [Parpola] does not choose them because they are not homophonous with the word for Murukan that he is looking for. I personally believe that if the Indus valley people were Dravidians, one of their gods was called Murukan. But he is hiding in still some other sign.[21]

Whatever the nuances of the Indus language issue, there can be no doubt of an inherent uncertainty in the interpretation of the Indus signs. Let us conclude with one last cautionary example. As already mentioned, virtually every scholar except Fairservis thinks that 𝄐 depicts a fish. But consider the disagreement about the most common Indus sign of all, ∪. To Parpola, it shows the head of a horned cow seen from the front; to Fairservis, a pot with handles; and to another scholar, Yuri Knorozov, a peepal tree. Each has his reasons. As Parpola was obliged to confess in the final words of his massively erudite study of the Indus script:

> Many of the signs . . . are so simplified and schematic that it is very difficult to understand their pictorial meaning unambiguously and objectively. Another drawback is the scantiness of the material . . . It looks most unlikely that the Indus script will ever be deciphered fully, unless radically different source material becomes available. That, however, must not deter us from trying.[22]

Parpola's assessment is honest, scientific and true, if unsensational. After all, it took well over a century to decipher the Mayan script, following several false starts and hiatuses. Indus script decipherers have been on the much barer and more ancient Indus trail for less than a century. If excavations in Pakistan and India continue in the future, and if they yield substantial new discoveries of inscriptions, especially a significantly longer text, I think there is a reasonable prospect of a widely accepted, if inevitably limited, Indus script decipherment. Whatever happens, one thing is surely beyond dispute: the Indus script will retain its unique status as the world's most deciphered script.

ELEVEN
INDUS ORIGINS OF HINDUISM?

S ome Indus seals and many Indus tablets depict crocodiles, which is not surprising given that the fish-eating crocodile known as the gharial is native to the Indian subcontinent. Sometimes the gharial is even shown with the 'fish' sign in its jaws (suggesting that this common sign sometimes took its most obvious pictographic meaning). More puzzling is a strange image painted on a Mature-period potsherd from Amri in Sindh of two crocodiles with a 'fish' sign. One of the crocodile images (the other is broken) has no hind legs; instead, what appears to be a bar projects from the back part of its body at a right angle, linking it with the centre of the image.

To explain this, Asko Parpola makes a plausible link with a unique crocodile cult still practised in some fifty tribal villages in southern Gujarat, as documented by two scholars in the early 1970s, though now rapidly declining. Parpola describes the cult's practices thus:

> Four- or eight-faceted images of crocodiles, normally a couple, are made of wood and installed on wooden posts. The installation ceremony celebrates their wedding, and the images are worshipped by smearing them with vermilion paste and with offerings of chicken or goats and milk or alcohol, afterwards consumed by the participants. The male crocodile can be substituted with a *lingam*-like post or the couple with a single crocodile having a head at either end.[1]

In return for their worship, people ask the crocodile gods for the usual kinds of boon desired in an Indian village: fertility and off-spring for women, milk and calves from cows, and help against drought, disease and sorcery.

These Gujarati villagers are Hindus, practising what is often termed as 'village' Hinduism. Typically this consists of a mother goddess as the guardian deity of the village, her husband or servant symbolized by a bull or buffalo, and worship in the form of clay or stone images and the cult of sacred trees with divine inhabitants. Very likely the same customs prevailed in Gujarati villages four thousand or five thousand years ago, given that the bull and the buffalo, the fish and the peacock, and fig trees, especially the peepal and the banyan, are important motifs on Indus painted pottery from both the Early and the Mature periods of the Indus civiliza-tion. All of its early excavators, beginning with Marshall, sensed the roots of Hinduism in the civilization, as we know; and so has almost every subsequent researcher. '[I] do not suggest that Hindu-ism in its modern form was present in the Indus civilisation, but some major elements of the Hindu belief system seem to be present in Indus finds', writes Chakrabarti. 'It is possible to trace some of the major elements of later Indian religions — especially in their devotional aspects such as goddess worship, tree worship, reverence

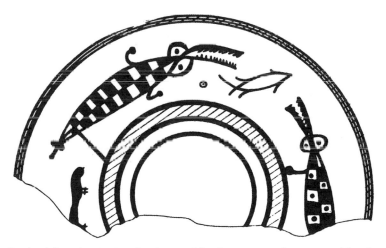

Potsherd from Amri painted with crocodiles. It appears to show a crocodile cult that has survived from the Mature Indus period to the present day.

for certain animals, etc. back to the Indus civilisation.'[2] But there is not much clarity about exactly which aspects of the civilization, especially the urban civilization, can legitimately be considered 'Hindu'.

Definite modern survivals from the ancient civilization include the swastika symbol; the Hindu female custom of applying vermilion paste, known as *sindoor*, to the middle parting of the hair to symbolize marriage, which has been identified in many Indus female figurines; libation vessels for dispensing milk and water in Hindu rituals, which are identical to hollowed-out and decorated Indus conch shells (*Turbinella pyrum*); and even the small water jar used for washing after using the toilet, known as a *lota*, which is commonly found in Indus commodes. Less certain, though probable, is phallus worship. At least one of the numerous stone objects identified by Marshall as potentially 'phallic' is unmistakably so; there are several clearly ithyphallic statuettes from Mohenjo-daro and Chanhu-daro; and a small terracotta object from Kalibangan

Tablet with five swastikas (above), a common motif in Indus art, made of terracotta, from Harappa. Swastikas appear throughout Indian history, for example in the swastika and lotus motifs of a pierced stone window in a 9th-century AD Hindu temple in south India (right).

Swastika on
the carved
wooden strut of
a contemporary
house in Gujarat.

is remarkably close to the shape of a typical present-day Shiva *lingam*
and its base. In addition, it is fairly easy to propose present-day
Hindu counterparts of some of the seal imagery, such as the worship of deities (probably female) in peepal trees, the yogic postures
of many figures and the depiction of 'proto Shiva' whatever doubts
may exist about the precise identity of this horned yogic figure.

On the other hand, specific rituals associated with rain and rivers,
which are so important in Hinduism, are not depicted on Indus
seals, despite the cities' preoccupation with rivers, water and, perhaps, ritual purity. Nor do the seals depict the monkey, despite the
widespread portrayal of the monkey god Hanuman in Hindu painting and sculpture. Also absent from the seals (though occasionally
depicted on terracotta tablets) are snakes, notwithstanding the

importance of the cobra in Hindu mythology and its popularity in performances of snake-charming, which is not depicted anywhere in Indus art. Moreover, both the seals and other archaeological discoveries show that the bull was a sacred animal, rather than the cow as in Hinduism: unlike the bull, the cow never appears on seals and was apparently sacrificed, judging from the cattle bones found in Indus 'fire altars'. As for dead humans, Indus corpses were generally buried, rather than cremated – again in telling contradistinction to standard practice among Hindus.

Such comparisons raise the perennial question of what defines Hinduism. Is it ethnicity, social customs, religious rituals, mythology, theology – or all of the above? The earliest use of 'Hindu' – dating to about 515 BC, when the Persian ruler Darius the Great annexed the Indus valley – was geographical, not religious: it derived from the Sanskrit word *sindhu*, meaning 'river', specifically the Indus river. The Persians dropped the 's' and used *hindu* to mean 'pertaining to the region of the Indus' – the area now known as Sindh. In a pioneering map of the world created in the second century AD by the Greek geographer Claudius Ptolemy, the approach to India from the west is marked 'Indiostena regio', Latin for 'region of Hindustan'. Thereafter, the Arabs, who conquered Sindh in the eighth century, gradually extended the meaning of the word so as to denote north India as 'Hindustan'.

During the first millennium AD most Indians – other than Buddhists and Jains – identified themselves by their caste or sect. 'The clubbing together of all the castes, non-castes and sects under one label – Hindu – would have been strange to most people and even repugnant to some, since it would have made Brahmins, Sudras and Untouchables equal members of a religious community of "Hindus"', observes a leading historian of pre-Muslim India, Romila Thapar. 'This was alien to the existing religions in the subcontinent.'[3] Not until the second millennium did 'Hindu' eventually acquire its current meaning connected with a group religious identity. The earliest use of the term in this sense came in the fourteenth century, though it was still infrequent, while its earliest citation in the *Oxford English Dictionary* is dated 1655, from the work of a British travel writer who visited the court of the Great Mughal:

This small Indus object made of terracotta, from Kalibangan, resembles a present-day Shiva *lingam*, the sacred phallic object used in Shiva worship. Coincidence, or evidence for the Indus roots of Hinduism?

'The Inhabitants in generall of Indostan were all antiently [anciently] Gentiles, called in generall Hindoes.' During the Mughal empire, in the seventeenth century, the British began to use 'Hindu' (or 'Hindoo') to describe all people living in the subcontinent. In the late eighteenth century, they extended the term to the religion of 'Hindooism'. By the nineteenth century, 'Hinduism' had become the general name for the native religions of India, excluding Buddhism, Jainism and Sikhism – both among the British and among Indians who opposed colonialism but wished to distinguish themselves from fellow Muslims. During the 1920s a Hindi word, *hindutva*, was coined (using the Sanskrit suffix *-tva*) to mean 'Hindu identity'; it appears in V. D. Savarkar's booklet, *Hindutva: Who is Hindu?*, first published in 1923 and now a key work among Hindu nationalists. Nevertheless, notes Parpola, 'Some Indians object to having a foreign term for their religion, preferring the Sanskrit expression *sanatana dharma*, "eternal law or truth", despite the fact that this expression was not applied to any religious system in ancient texts' – including the most ancient, the Vedic texts.[4]

This objection reminds us that the above historical background, necessary as it is, entirely overlooks the basis for the many different traditions of worship, or sects, within Hinduism itself, such as Shaivism (the worship of Shiva) and Vaishnavism (the worship of Vishnu). Each tradition has its own theology and rituals, which are as distinct from each other among Hindus as, say, Catholicism and Protestantism are among Christians. These 'classical' traditions date from much later than the Vedic period – probably from the time of the composition of the Hindu epics, the *Mahabharata* and the *Ramayana*, which began around 300 BC. But many of the 'classical' gods date back, at least in part, to the pantheon of the much older Vedic religion.

The principal Vedic gods are beings known as *devas*, the 'shining ones', and not surprisingly they are associated mostly with the sky and the heavens, rather than with the soil, animals and the mysteries of fertility – the province of 'village' Hinduism. The union of the Vedic Sky Father, Dyaus Pitar (compare Greek Zeus Pater, Latin Jupiter), with Mother Earth provides the earliest creation myth in the Rigveda. But we do not hear much about Dyaus, whose place is taken by Varuna, guardian of the sacred law and cosmic order (*rita*). Varuna, with his thousand eyes ever watchful for wrongdoing, is one of the Vedic gods who always behaves ethically. But then Varuna, in his turn, gives way to Prajapati, the Lord of Creatures,

'Vishnu as Matsya killing the demon Shankhasura and rescuing the four Vedas', painted *c.* 1760. The Vedas stand at the top left of the painting.

who, in the form of the Primeval Man, is dismembered to form the phenomenal world, including the four main castes. Other gods include Mitra, the god of integrity and friendship, who is closely linked with Varuna; Surya, the sun god; Agni, the god of fire, who consumes sacrificial offerings and thereby conveys them from men to the gods; Soma, who is both a god and an elixir of immortality, *soma* (as mentioned earlier); and in the afterlife, Yama, the god of death, who presides over the spirits of the dead. There are also important goddesses, such as the goddesses of Earth, the dawn (Ushas) and speech (Vac). Most important of all, however, is the warrior Indra, god of war and god of weather, with many of the characteristics of Zeus and Thor, as shown in his exploits. Indra kills the demon Vritra by wielding his thunderbolt, and thereby releases the waters of life. He rescues the sun from another demon (possibly a reference to a solar eclipse) with the help of the high priest. He also destroys the fortresses of the enemy known as the Dasas (as cited by Wheeler). He is borne by an eagle to heaven and returns with *soma* for men and gods. And he regularly overdoes the drinking of *soma* in noisy wassails.

Many of the gods' names first seen in the Rigveda continue in 'classical' Hinduism, for example Varuna, Surya, Agni, Yama and Indra, though with varying degrees of importance attached to them compared to their Vedic originals. But there is little sign in the Vedic pantheon of the two greatest gods of later Hinduism: Shiva and Vishnu. In fact, Shiva is not mentioned by name. The Vedic storm god, Rudra, 'in whom are later incorporated other ideas in the Hindu conception of Shiva, is a turbulent god more to be propitiated than petitioned', notes the Indo-Aryan specialist Thomas Trautmann. Vishnu, though mentioned by name, is merely 'a dwarf who with three giant strides wins the earth, air and sky for the gods and consigns the demons to the nether world'.[5] Indeed, few of the Vedic deities became the major gods and goddesses of Hinduism, and only one of the major deities, Surya, kept a central position in later Hindu art as a dynastic deity. Objectively viewed, there is really no great connection between the Vedic gods and the gods of modern Hinduism, despite the high regard for the Vedas among current Hindus.

'The Vedic contribution to Hinduism, especially Hindu cult-practice and speculation, is not a large one; Vedic influence on mythology is rather stronger, though here also there has been a profound regeneration', the eminent Indologist Louis Renou observed more than half a century ago. 'Even in those cases where continuity has been suggested, as for Rudra-Shiva, the differences are really far more striking than the similarities.'[6]

This surprising fact immediately begs a question: where did the non-Vedic elements of 'classical' Hinduism come from? Many of them must have evolved in the centuries of the post-Vedic period up to the presumed completion of the *Mahabharata* in its present form (around AD 400), or been assimilated from local religious cults (such as the crocodile cult in Gujarat). But some of them should date back to the Indus civilization, suggested Renou. 'If the forms of religion revealed in the seals and figurines of the Indus have any remote connection with Indian forms, it is not so much with those of Vedism as with those of Hinduism, a Hinduism which, though known to us only by inference, must have already existed in Vedic times, and probably considerably earlier.'[7]

If this inference is correct, then the origins of 'classical' Hinduism most likely lie both in the Indus civilization and in the Vedic culture. The latter developed independently and strongly differed from the former. But during the second millennium BC – the period of Indus decline and Indo-Aryan migrations – the disparate customs, rituals and mythology of the Indus civilization and the Vedic culture probably mingled and fused to form the foundation of the 'classical' Hinduism that undoubtedly gave rise to modern Hinduism.

Just how different the Indus civilization was from the Vedic culture emerges from the basic content-matter of the Rigveda. This makes very occasional reference to villages, but none at all to towns and cities; it contains references to crafts such as weaving and leatherwork, but none to brickmaking and jewellery making; there are infrequent references to iron (which was unknown to the Indus civilization), but none to metallurgy or mining; and there are a few references to journeys and even to boats and ships (though the ships are probably metaphorical), but none at all to merchants and trade, whether long-distance or not – not to mention no references to complex weights and measures. Moreover, the Rigveda mentions defensive armour and the horse in its descriptions of warfare and sacrifice. Yet, evidence for armour or war is absent from the Indus civilization, and so is the horse, as we know. Beyond reasonable dispute, the overwhelming majority of the Rigveda's verses concern sacrifices, rituals and gods, generally named, with many references to nature and natural phenomena, creation, women, animals (especially cows and horses), pastoral life, chariots, war and death.

The above comparative catalogue more or less disproves, amongst other things, that the Indus civilization might have been the progenitor of the Vedic culture, or indeed vice versa. For how could one explain, assuming the first scenario, a development from massive brick-built urban architecture to virtually no architecture, or, assuming the second, the prominence of armour and the horse followed by their disappearance? If the Vedic culture gave rise to the Indus civilization, which then gave rise to 'classical' Hinduism, then the cow would have had to pass from sacred to profane and then back to sacred. As Marshall was the first to note, 'from whatever angle we view these civilisations, it is impossible to discover for them a common source, or to explain their divergent characters on any hypothesis other than that the Vedic was not only the later of the two, but that it had an independent invention.'[8]

This is not to say that the culture of the Indus civilization was entirely unlike that of the Vedic period. For example, the Indus people gambled. Many of their clay gaming boards and dice made of simple split reeds, cowrie shells, clay and stone cubes, and finely carved ivory rods with circles incised on each face, have been excavated. And so did the Vedic people, as described in the following verses, seven and eight, of the Rigveda's powerful 'Gambler's Lament' (in Wendy Doniger O'Flaherty's translation):

The dice goad like hooks and prick like whips; they enslave, deceive and torment. They give presents as children do, striking back at the winners. They are coated with honey – an irresistible power over the gambler. / Their army, three bands of fifty,

Game pieces from Mohenjo-daro suggest that gambling was commonplace during the Indus civilization.

plays by rules as immutable as those of the god Savitr [god of the rising and setting sun]. They do not bow even to the wrath of those whose power is terrifying; the king himself bows down before them.[9]

In addition, the Vedic people probably lived in small settlements, practised some degree of agriculture (ploughs are occasionally referred to), employed carpenters and metalworkers to make and repair their wheeled chariots, fashioned precious adornments for their women and supported traders who made journeys from village to village. But these things and activities were not sufficiently extensive or permanent to leave behind any remains today, or at least nothing that archaeologists have yet discovered – except for the Vedic peoples' oral literature. However much Hindu nationalists may desire there to be a strong Vedic–Indus resemblance, no amount of special pleading about the silence of the Vedic scriptures on secular matters can marry up the society described in the Vedas with the material culture of the Indus civilization.

Where does this situation leave the origins of Hinduism? In a word, tangled. For, as we know, the Indus civilization was not *sui generis*; it was influenced by the cultures of Mesopotamia. And the same may be said of the Vedic culture; it absorbed words from the Dravidian languages, and presumably also elements of Dravidian religion. Parpola, who has devoted a lifetime to disentangling all of these influences through imaginative study of languages, scripts, art and surviving customs, argues:

> It is reasonable to expect that historical South Asia has preserved Harappan [i.e. Indus] traditions. Late Harappan people outnumbered Indo-Aryan-speaking immigrants. Fusion of these principal population groups continued for many centuries with mixed marriages and growing bilingualism. Newcomers' need to deal with the majority population gave local leaders and priests a chance to act as middlemen and obtain positions in the emerging new social order.[10]

The Indus archaeological remains speak to the eye – yet the Indus people remain silent. The Vedic culture is full of sound and feeling – yet it exists solely on the printed page. Until the Indus signs are made to speak, 'proto-Shiva' must continue to be a most intriguing, but unverifiable, Indus ancestor of one of the primary forms of God in modern Hinduism.

TWELVE
THE INDUS
INHERITANCE

In *The Discovery of India*, published the year before he became India's prime minister in 1947, Jawaharlal Nehru wrote memorably of his personal encounters with the Indus civilization in 1931 and 1936, as follows:

> I stood on a mound of Mohenjo-daro in the Indus valley in the northwest of India, and all around me lay the houses and streets of this ancient city that is said to have existed over five thousand years ago . . . Astonishing thought: that any culture or civilisation should have this continuity for five or six thousand years or more; and not in a static, unchanging sense, for India was changing and progressing all the time. She was coming into intimate contact with the Persians, the Egyptians, the Greeks, the Chinese, the Arabs, the Central Asians, and the peoples of the Mediterranean. But though she influenced them and was influenced by them, her cultural basis was strong enough to endure. What was the secret of this strength? Where did it come from? . . . It was, surprisingly enough, a predominantly secular civilisation, and the religious element, though present, did not dominate the scene . . . [At] this dawn of India's story, she does not appear as a puling infant, but already grown up in many ways. She is not oblivious of life's ways, lost in dreams of a vague and unrealisable supernatural world, but has made considerable technical progress in the arts and amenities of life, creating not only things of beauty, but also the utilitarian and more

typical emblems of modern civilisation – good baths and drainage systems.[1]

Evidently Nehru, though a nationalist at the political level, was intellectually and emotionally drawn to the Indus civilization by his regard for internationalism, secularism, art, technology and modernity.

By contrast, Nehru's political rival, Muhammad Ali Jinnah, the founder of Pakistan, neither visited Mohenjo-daro nor commented on the significance of the Indus civilization. Nor did Nehru's mentor, Mohandas Karamchand Gandhi, India's greatest nationalist leader. In Jinnah's case, this silence is puzzling, given that the Indus valley lies in Pakistan and, moreover, Jinnah himself was born in Karachi, in the province of Sindh, not so far from Mohenjo-daro. In Gandhi's case, the silence is even more puzzling. Not only was Gandhi, too, an Indus dweller, so to speak, having been born in Gujarat, in Saurashtra, but he must surely also have become aware in the 1930s of the Indus civilization as the potential origin of Hinduism, plus the astonishing revelation that it apparently functioned without resort to military violence. Yet, there is not a single comment on the Indus civilization in the one hundred large volumes of the *Collected Works of Mahatma Gandhi*. The nearest he comes to commenting is a touching remark recorded by the Mahatma's secretary when the two of them visited the site of Marshall's famous excavations at Taxila, in northern Punjab, in 1938. On being shown a pair of heavy silver ancient anklets by the curator of the Taxila archaeological museum, 'Gandhiji with a deep sigh remarked: "Just like what my mother used to wear."'[2]

It would not be much of an exaggeration to say that the enthusiasm of Nehru and the indifference of Jinnah and Gandhi established a pattern for the response to the Indus civilization in the decades following the political independence of the subcontinent. Since its Indo-British discovery in the 1920s, it has stirred the keenest interest internationally, rather than nationally, that is, among European, American and Japanese archaeologists and linguists, who have taken the lead in excavating and interpreting the civilization. In many cases, they have collaborated fruitfully with archaeologists from Pakistan and from India – but with a few distinguished exceptions from both countries, such as Rafique Mughal and Iravatham Mahadevan, the impetus towards greater understanding has come from abroad, not from Pakistan and India.

Certainly part of the problem is that the international border, with its history of political tension, has divided the field of study since 1947, physically and academically. However, in addition there has been a psychological difficulty on both sides. The majority of Pakistanis have not, it seems, come to regard the Indus civilization as a key part of their heritage (though Mohenjo-daro is shown on one of the Pakistani currency notes) – perhaps in somewhat the same way that present-day Egyptians do not really relate to the civilization of the ancient Egyptians. On the other side, the majority of Indians prefer, like Gandhi, to devote their attention to the Vedic culture, the Indo-Aryans and the subsequent epics of Hindu civilization. Hence this lament by the archaeologist Chakrabarti at the start of his academic collection, *Indus Civilization Sites in India: New Discoveries*, published in 2004:

> If Indian school and university history textbooks are anything to go by, the Indus civilisation hardly plays a role in the historical consciousness of the nation. An insignificant position in the curriculum and hopelessly disjointed writings are characteristic of the Indian academic approach to this civilisation. And yet, there ought to be a far more focused interest in this largest of Bronze Age civilisations of the third millennium BC, which is firmly rooted in the Indian subcontinent and has contributed fundamentally to the formation of India as we know it today. The still undeciphered Indus script denies us ready access to contemporary ideas and discourses, but the excavated remains go a long way to show how this civilisation rose, flourished and declined to eventually become a part of the cultural flow of the subcontinent as a whole.[3]

One hopes that in the decades to come, this plea will not fall on deaf ears in India. Along with Nehru, Indians can legitimately take pride in the fact that the Indus civilization was essentially indigenous, like the civilizations of the ancient Sumerians and Egyptians.

Nonetheless, the Indus civilization is far from being lost. Though located in Pakistan and India, it belongs to the world, as John Marshall announced in the *Illustrated London News* in 1924, and as Kenneth Clark reminded the world in his *Civilisation* in 1969. In 1980 Mohenjo-daro was inscribed in the list of World Heritage Sites by UNESCO. The Indus civilization's half-understood mysteries continue to fascinate anyone interested in the origins of civilization. Personally, I am drawn to what appears to be its success in combining artistic excellence, technological sophistication and economic vigour with social egalitarianism, political freedom and religious moderation over more than half a millennium. If further investigation were to show this attractive picture to be accurate, the Indus civilization would also be a hopeful sign for the future of humankind.

REFERENCES

1 AN ENIGMATIC WORLD

1 Kenneth Clark, *Civilisation: A Personal View* (London, 1969), p. 33.
2 Mortimer Wheeler, *The Indus Civilization*, 3rd edn (Cambridge, 1968), p. 101.
3 Jane McIntosh, *A Peaceful Realm: The Rise and Fall of the Indus Civilization* (Boulder, CO, 2002), p. 50.
4 John Marshall, *Mohenjo-daro and the Indus Civilization* (London, 1931), p. vii.
5 Jawaharlal Nehru, *The Discovery of India* (London, 1946), p. 49.
6 N. Jha and N. S. Rajaram, *The Deciphered Indus Script: Methodology, Readings, Interpretations* (New Delhi, 2000), p. 254.
7 Ibid., p. 162.
8 Ibid., p. 152.
9 Iravatham Mahadevan, 'One Sees What One Wants To', *Frontline*, 11–24 November 2000.
10 Michael Witzel and Steve Farmer, 'Horseplay in Harappa: The Indus Valley Decipherment Hoax', *Frontline*, 30 September–13 October 2000.
11 Jonathan Mark Kenoyer, *Ancient Cities of the Indus Valley Civilization* (Karachi, 1998), p. 30.
12 Marshall, *Mohenjo-daro*, p. 2.
13 Stuart Piggott, *Prehistoric India to 1000 BC* (London, 1950), p. 67.

2 DISCOVERY

1 John Marshall, 'First Light on a Long-forgotten Civilisation: New Discoveries of an Unknown Prehistoric Past in India', *Illustrated London News*, 20 September 1924.
2 Charles Masson, *Narrative of Various Journeys in Balochistan, Afghanistan, and the Punjab*, vol. 1 (London, 1842), pp. 452–3.
3 Alexander Cunningham, *Annual Report of the Archaeological Survey of India*, v (Calcutta, 1875), p. 108.
4 Asko Parpola, 'New Light on "Major Clark"', in *Corpus of Indus Seals and Inscriptions*, vol. III: *New Material, Untraced Objects, and Collections*

Outside India and Pakistan, ed. Asko Parpola, B. M. Pande and Petteri Koskikallio (Helsinki, 2010), p. lx.

5 Quoted in Nayanjot Lahiri, *Finding Forgotten Cities: How the Indus Civilization was Discovered* (Oxford, 2006), p. 100.

6 Quoted ibid., p. 172.

7 Quoted ibid.

8 Quoted ibid., p. 177.

9 Quoted ibid., p. 189.

10 Quoted ibid., p. 248.

11 John Marshall, *Mohenjo-daro and the Indus Civilization* (London, 1931), p. 91.

12 Marshall, 'First Light on a Long-forgotten Civilisation'.

13 John Marshall, *Annual Report of the Archaeological Survey of India, 1925–26: Exploration, Western Circle, Mohenjo daro* (Calcutta, 1926), p. 75.

14 Asko Parpola, *Deciphering the Indus Script* (Cambridge, 1994), p. 21.

15 Dilip K. Chakrabarti, ed., *Indus Civilization Sites in India: New Discoveries* (Mumbai, 2004), p. 11.

16 Hans J. Nissen, 'Early Civilizations in the Near and Middle East', in *Forgotten Cities on the Indus: Early Civilization in Pakistan from the 8th to the 2nd Millennium BC*, ed. Michael Jansen, Máire Mulloy and Günter Urban (Mainz, 1991), p. 33.

17 Stuart Piggott, *Prehistoric India to 1000 BC* (London, 1950), pp. 133, 136, 138, 201.

18 Mortimer Wheeler, *Still Digging: Interleaves from an Antiquary's Notebook* (London, 1955), p. 192.

19 Quoted in Gregory L. Possehl, *The Indus Civilization: A Contemporary Perspective* (New Delhi, 2003), p. 238.

20 Possehl, *The Indus Civilization*, p. 19.

21 Rita P. Wright, *The Ancient Indus: Urbanism, Economy, and Society* (Cambridge, 2010), p. 95.

22 Mortimer Wheeler, *The Indus Civilization*, 3rd edn (Cambridge, 1968), p. 125.

23 Marshall, *Mohenjo-daro*, p. viii.

24 Jean-François Jarrige, 'Mehrgarh: Its Place in the Development of Ancient Cultures in Pakistan', in *Forgotten Cities on the Indus*, ed. Jansen, Mulloy and Urban, p. 36.

25 Ibid., p. 49.

26 Günter Urban, 'The Indus Civilization: The Story of a Discovery', in *Forgotten Cities on the Indus*, ed. Jansen, Mulloy and Urban, pp. 25–6.

27 Wright, *The Ancient Indus*, pp. 114–15.

3 Architecture

1 John Marshall, *Mohenjo-daro and the Indus Civilization* (London, 1931), p. 6.
2 Ibid., p. 286.
3 Ibid., p. 25.
4 Jonathan Mark Kenoyer, *Ancient Cities of the Indus Valley Civilization* (Karachi, 1998), p. 57.
5 Marshall, *Mohenjo-daro*, p. 15.
6 Mortimer Wheeler, *Still Digging: Interleaves from an Antiquary's Notebook* (London, 1955), p. 192.
7 Kenoyer, *Ancient Cities of the Indus Valley Civilization*, p. 56.
8 Massimo Vidale, 'Crafts and Skills in Mohenjo-daro', in *Forgotten Cities on the Indus: Early Civilization in Pakistan from the 8th to the 2nd Millennium BC*, ed. Michael Jansen, Máire Mulloy and Günter Urban (Mainz, 1991), p. 214.
9 Gregory L. Possehl, *The Indus Civilization: A Contemporary Perspective* (New Delhi, 2003), p. 212.
10 Wheeler, *Still Digging*, p. 225.
11 Kenoyer, *Ancient Cities of the Indus Valley Civilization*, p. 64.
12 Jane R. McIntosh, *The Ancient Indus Valley: New Perspectives* (Santa Barbara, CA, 2008), pp. 276–7.
13 Rita P. Wright, *The Ancient Indus: Urbanism, Economy, and Society* (Cambridge, 2010), p. 122.
14 Michael Jansen, 'Mohenjo-daro – a City on the Indus', in *Forgotten Cities on the Indus*, ed. Jansen, Mulloy and Urban, p. 161.
15 Kenoyer, *Ancient Cities of the Indus Valley Civilization*, p. 61.
16 Marshall, *Mohenjo-daro*, p. 263.
17 Stuart Piggott, *Prehistoric India to 1000 BC* (London, 1950), p. 168.
18 Marshall, *Mohenjo-daro*, p. 75.
19 Kenoyer, *Ancient Cities of the Indus Valley Civilization*, p. 120.

4 Arts and Crafts

1 Mortimer Wheeler, *The Indus Civilization*, 3rd edn (Cambridge, 1968), p. 101.
2 George F. Dales, 'The Phenomenon of the Indus Civilisation', in *Forgotten Cities on the Indus: Early Civilization in Pakistan from the 8th to the 2nd Millennium BC*, ed. Michael Jansen, Máire Mulloy and Günter Urban (Mainz, 1991), p. 133.
3 Jonathan Mark Kenoyer, *Ancient Cities of the Indus Valley Civilization* (Karachi, 1998), p. 96.
4 Asko Parpola, *Deciphering the Indus Script* (Cambridge, 1994), p. 8.
5 Kenoyer, *Ancient Cities of the Indus Valley Civilization*, p. 98.
6 Ibid., p. 159.
7 Ibid., p. 162.
8 Ibid., p. 138.

9 Ibid., p. 161.
10 Jane McIntosh, *A Peaceful Realm: The Rise and Fall of the Indus Civilization* (Boulder, CO, 2002), p. 136.
11 John Marshall, *Mohenjo-daro and the Indus Civilization* (London, 1931), p. 33.
12 Ibid., p. vii.
13 Stuart Piggott, *Prehistoric India to 1000 BC* (London, 1950), p. 183.
14 Kenoyer, *Ancient Cities of the Indus Valley Civilization*, p. 73.

5 AGRICULTURE

1 Jane R. McIntosh, *The Ancient Indus Valley: New Perspectives* (Santa Barbara, CA, 2008), p. 109.
2 Richard Meadow, 'The Domestication and Exploitation of Plants and Animals in the Greater Indus Valley, 7th–2nd Millennium BC', in *Forgotten Cities on the Indus: Early Civilization in Pakistan from the 8th to the 2nd Millennium BC*, ed. Michael Jansen, Máire Mulloy and Günter Urban (Mainz, 1991), p. 51.
3 John Marshall, *Mohenjo-daro and the Indus Civilization* (London, 1931), p. 389.
4 Gregory L. Possehl, *The Indus Civilization: A Contemporary Perspective* (New Delhi, 2003), p. 64.
5 McIntosh, *The Ancient Indus Valley*, p. 113.
6 Dilip K. Chakrabarti, ed., *Indus Civilization Sites in India: New Discoveries* (Mumbai, 2004), p. 18.
7 McIntosh, *The Ancient Indus Valley*, p. 121.
8 Jonathan Mark Kenoyer, *Ancient Cities of the Indus Valley Civilization* (Karachi, 1998), p. 164.
9 R. B. Seymour Sewell and B. S. Guha, 'Zoological Remains', in Marshall, *Mohenjo-daro*, p. 651.
10 McIntosh, *The Ancient Indus Valley*, p. 132.
11 Kenoyer, *Ancient Cities of the Indus Valley Civilization*, p. 169.

6 TRADE

1 Maurizio Tosi, 'The Indus Civilisation beyond the Indian Subcontinent', in *Forgotten Cities on the Indus: Early Civilization in Pakistan from the 8th to the 2nd Millennium BC*, ed. Michael Jansen, Máire Mulloy and Günter Urban (Mainz, 1991), p. 123.
2 Jonathan Mark Kenoyer, *Ancient Cities of the Indus Valley Civilization* (Karachi, 1998), p. 99.
3 Ibid., p. 89.
4 Thor Heyerdahl, *The Tigris Expedition: In Search of Our Beginnings* (London, 1980), p. 266.
5 Brian Fagan, *Beyond the Blue Horizon: How the Earliest Mariners Unlocked the Secrets of the Oceans* (London, 2012), p. 122.

6 Jane R. McIntosh, *The Ancient Indus Valley: New Perspectives* (Santa Barbara, CA, 2008), p. 86.

7 Shereen Ratnagar, *Trading Encounters: From the Euphrates to the Indus in the Bronze Age* (New Delhi, 2004), p. 250.

8 Tosi, 'The Indus Civilisation beyond the Indian Subcontinent', p. 116.

9 Hans J. Nissen, 'Early Civilizations in the Near and Middle East', in *Forgotten Cities on the Indus*, ed. Jansen, Mulloy and Urban, p. 30.

10 Quoted in Tosi, 'The Indus Civilisation beyond the Indian Subcontinent', p. 120.

11 Kenoyer, *Ancient Cities of the Indus Valley Civilization*, p. 97.

12 Leonard Woolley, *Ur 'of the Chaldees'*, ed. P.R.S. Moorey (London, 1982), p. 132.

13 Rita P. Wright, *The Ancient Indus: Urbanism, Economy, and Society* (Cambridge, 2010), p. 225.

14 Kenoyer, *Ancient Cities of the Indus Valley Civilization*, p. 98.

15 Asko Parpola, 'Indus Civilisation', in *Brill's Encyclopaedia of Hinduism*, ed. Knut A. Jacobsen, vol. IV (Leiden, 2012), p. 6.

16 John Marshall, *Mohenjo-daro and the Indus Civilization* (London, 1931), pp. 463–4.

17 Jane McIntosh, *A Peaceful Realm: The Rise and Fall of the Indus Civilization* (Boulder, CO, 2002), p. 175.

7 SOCIETY

1 Leonard Woolley, *Ur 'of the Chaldees'*, ed. P.R.S. Moorey (London, 1982), pp. 76–8, 80.

2 Asko Parpola, 'Indus Civilisation', in *Brill's Encyclopaedia of Hinduism*, ed. Knut A. Jacobsen, vol. IV (Leiden, 2012), p. 5.

3 Gregory L. Possehl, *The Indus Civilization: A Contemporary Perspective* (New Delhi, 2003), p. 57.

4 Dilip K. Chakrabarti, ed., *Indus Civilization Sites in India: New Discoveries* (Mumbai, 2004), pp. 16–17.

5 Rita P. Wright, *The Ancient Indus: Urbanism, Economy, and Society* (Cambridge, 2010), p. 127.

6 Jonathan Mark Kenoyer, *Ancient Cities of the Indus Valley Civilization* (Karachi, 1998), p. 117.

7 Jane R. McIntosh, *The Ancient Indus Valley: New Perspectives* (Santa Barbara, CA, 2008), p. 268.

8 Ibid., p. 269.

9 Kenoyer, *Ancient Cities of the Indus Valley Civilization*, p. 83.

10 Jane McIntosh, *A Peaceful Realm: The Rise and Fall of the Indus Civilization* (Boulder, CO, 2002), p. 129.

11 Possehl, *The Indus Civilization*, p. 174.

12 Kenoyer, *Ancient Cities of the Indus Valley Civilization*, p. 124.

13 Ibid., p. 82.

14 Ibid., p. 102.
15 Chakrabarti, ed., *Indus Civilization Sites in India*, p. 17.

8 RELIGION

1 John Marshall, *Mohenjo-daro and the Indus Civilization* (London, 1931), p. 284.
2 Gregory L. Possehl, *The Indus Civilization: A Contemporary Perspective* (New Delhi, 2003), p. 152.
3 Quoted in Asko Parpola, *Deciphering the Indus Script* (Cambridge, 1994), p. 221.
4 Jane McIntosh, *A Peaceful Realm: The Rise and Fall of the Indus Civilization* (Boulder, CO, 2002), p. 121.
5 Catherine Jarrige, 'The Terracotta Figurines from Mehrgarh', in *Forgotten Cities on the Indus: Early Civilization in Pakistan from the 8th to the 2nd Millennium BC*, ed. Michael Jansen, Máire Mulloy and Günter Urban (Mainz, 1991), p. 92.
6 Marshall, *Mohenjo-daro*, p. 52.
7 Ibid., p. 53.
8 A. L. Basham, *The Origins and Development of Classical Hinduism* (Boston, MA, 1989), p. 4.
9 Jonathan Mark Kenoyer, *Ancient Cities of the Indus Valley Civilization* (Karachi, 1998), p. 86.
10 Marshall, *Mohenjo-daro*, p. 65.
11 Kenoyer, *Ancient Cities of the Indus Valley Civilization*, p. 119.
12 Quoted in Andrew Robinson, *The Story of Writing: Alphabets, Hieroglyphs and Pictograms*, revd edn (London, 2007), p. 121.

9 DECLINE AND DISAPPEARANCE

1 Gregory L. Possehl, *The Indus Civilization: A Contemporary Perspective* (New Delhi, 2003), pp. 243, 245.
2 Jonathan Mark Kenoyer, *Ancient Cities of the Indus Valley Civilization* (Karachi, 1998), p. 173.
3 Maurizio Tosi, 'The Indus Civilisation beyond the Indian Subcontinent', in *Forgotten Cities on the Indus: Early Civilization in Pakistan from the 8th to the 2nd Millennium BC*, ed. Michael Jansen, Máire Mulloy and Günter Urban (Mainz, 1991), p. 127.
4 Possehl, *The Indus Civilization*, p. 86.
5 Asko Parpola, *Deciphering the Indus Script* (Cambridge, 1994), p. 24.
6 Kenoyer, *Ancient Cities of the Indus Valley Civilization*, p. 183.
7 George F. Dales, 'The Phenomenon of the Indus Civilisation', in *Forgotten Cities on the Indus*, ed. Jansen, Mulloy and Urban, p. 144.
8 L. Flam, 'Fluvial Geomorphology of the Lower Indus Basin (Sindh, Pakistan) and the Indus Civilisation', in *Himalayas to the Sea: Geology,*

Geomorphology and the Quaternary, ed. J. F. Shroder Jr (New York, 1993), p. 287.

9   Jane McIntosh, *A Peaceful Realm: The Rise and Fall of the Indus Civilization* (Boulder, CO, 2002), p. 190.

10 Edward Simpson, *The Political Biography of an Earthquake: Aftermath and Amnesia in Gujarat, India* (London, 2013), p. 237.

11 Possehl, *The Indus Civilization*, p. 235.

12 Asko Parpola, 'Indus Civilisation', in *Brill's Encyclopaedia of Hinduism*, ed. Knut A. Jacobsen, vol. IV (Leiden, 2012), p. 7.

13 Eric H. Cline, *1177 BC: The Year Civilization Collapsed* (Princeton, NJ, 2014), p. 174.

14 McIntosh, *A Peaceful Realm*, p. 193.

10 Deciphering the Indus Script

1   John DeFrancis, *Visible Speech: The Diverse Oneness of Writing Systems* (Honolulu, 1989), p. 4.

2   Michael D. Coe, 'On *Not* Breaking the Indus Code', *Antiquity*, LXIX (1995), pp. 393–5.

3   Gregory Possehl, *Indus Age: The Writing System* (Philadelphia, PA, 1996), p. 101.

4   Asko Parpola, *Deciphering the Indus Script* (Cambridge, 1994), p. 57.

5   Possehl, *Indus Age*, p. 89.

6   Flinders Petrie, 'Mohenjo-daro', *Ancient Egypt and the East*, II (1932), p. 34.

7   J. V. Kinnier Wilson, 'Fish Rations and the Indus Script: Some New Arguments in the Case for Accountancy', *South Asian Studies*, III (1987), pp. 41–6.

8   S. R. Rao, *The Decipherment of the Indus Script* (Bombay, 1982), fig. 8.

9   Possehl, *Indus Age*, p. 168; Walter A. Fairservis Jr, *The Harappan Civilization and Its Writing: A Model for the Decipherment of the Indus Script* (Leiden, 1992), preface.

10 Iravatham Mahadevan, 'What do we Know about the Indus Script? *Neti Neti* ("Not This Nor That")', *Journal of the Institute of Asian Studies*, VII (1989), p. 9.

11 Ibid.

12 Steven Christopher Bonta, 'Topics in the Study of the Indus Valley Script', MA thesis, Department of Linguistics, Brigham Young University, Provo, Utah, 1996.

13 Parpola, *Deciphering the Indus Script*, p. 69.

14 Ibid., p. 82.

15 Ibid., p. 83.

16 Mahadevan, 'What do we Know about the Indus Script?', p. 11.

17 John Marshall, *Mohenjo-daro and the Indus Civilization* (London, 1931), p. 42.

18 Parpola, *Deciphering the Indus Script*, p. 165.

19 Quoted in Parpola, *Deciphering the Indus Script*, p. 181.
20 Iravatham Mahadevan, '"An Encyclopedia of the Indus Script"', *The Book Review*, 19 (1995), p. 11.
21 Interview with Iravatham Mahadevan, section 12, available at www.harappa.com.
22 Parpola, *Deciphering the Indus Script*, p. 278.

11 INDUS ORIGINS OF HINDUISM?

1   Asko Parpola, 'Indus Civilisation', in *Brill's Encyclopaedia of Hinduism*, ed. Knut A. Jacobsen, vol. IV (Leiden, 2012), p. 9.
2   Dilip K. Chakrabarti, ed., *Indus Civilization Sites in India: New Discoveries* (Mumbai, 2004), p. 20.
3   Romila Thapar, *Early India: From the Origins to AD 1300* (London, 2002), p. 439.
4   Asko Parpola, *The Roots of Hinduism: The Early Aryans and the Indus Civilization* (New York, 2015), p. 3.
5   Thomas R. Trautmann, *India: Brief History of a Civilization* (New York, 2011), p. 33.
6   Louis Renou, *Religions of Ancient India* (London, 1953), p. 47.
7   Ibid., p. 3.
8   John Marshall, *Mohenjo-daro and the Indus Civilization* (London, 1931), p. 112.
9   *The Rig Veda*, trans. Wendy Doniger O'Flaherty (London, 1981), p. 240.
10 Parpola, 'Indus Civilisation', p. 9.

12 THE INDUS INHERITANCE

1   Jawaharlal Nehru, *The Discovery of India* (London, 1946), pp. 30, 47, 49.
2   Pyarelal, *Mahatma Gandhi*, vol. I: *The Early Phase* (Ahmedabad, 1965), p. 192.
3   Dilip K. Chakrabarti, ed., *Indus Civilization Sites in India: New Discoveries* (Mumbai, 2004), p. 7.

■■ BIBLIOGRAPHY

Ameri, Marta, Sarah Kielt Costello, Gregg Jamison and Sarah Jarmer Scott, eds,
 *Seals and Sealing in the Ancient World: Case Studies from the Near East,
 Egypt, the Aegean, and South Asia* (Cambridge, 2018)

Aruz, Joan, ed., with Ronald Wallenfels, *Art of the First Cities: The Third
 Millennium B.C. from the Mediterranean to the Indus* (New Haven, CT, 2003)

Basham, A. L., *The Origins and Development of Classical Hinduism* (Boston,
 MA, 1989)

Bonta, Steven Christopher, 'Topics in the Study of the Indus Valley Script',
 MA thesis, Department of Linguistics, Brigham Young University, Provo,
 Utah, 1996

Chakrabarti, Dilip K., ed., *Indus Civilization Sites in India: New Discoveries*
 (Mumbai, 2004)

——, *The Oxford Companion to Indian Archaeology: The Archaeological
 Foundations of Ancient India, Stone Age to AD 13th Century* (New Delhi, 2006)

Clark, Kenneth, *Civilisation: A Personal View* (London, 1969)

Cline, Eric H., *1177 BC: The Year Civilization Collapsed* (Princeton, NJ, 2014)

Coe, Michael D., 'On *Not* Breaking the Indus Code', *Antiquity*, LXIX (1995),
 pp. 393–5

Coningham, Robin, and Ruth Young, *The Archaeology of South Asia: From the
 Indus to Asoka, c. 6500 BCE–200 CE* (New York, 2015)

Cunningham, Alexander, *Annual Report of the Archaeological Survey of India*,
 V (Calcutta, 1875)

DeFrancis, John, *Visible Speech: The Diverse Oneness of Writing Systems*
 (Honolulu, HI, 1989)

Dixit, Yama, David A. Hodell and Cameron A. Petrie, 'Abrupt Weakening of
 the Summer Monsoon in Northwest India ≈ 4100 yr Ago', *Geology*, XLII
 (2014), pp. 339–42

Doniger O'Flaherty, Wendy, trans., *The Rig Veda: An Anthology* (London, 1981)

Fagan, Brian, *Beyond the Blue Horizon: How the Earliest Mariners Unlocked
 the Secrets of the Oceans* (London, 2012)

Fairservis, Jr, Walter A., *The Harappan Civilization and its Writing: A Model
 for the Decipherment of the Indus Script* (Leiden, 1992)

Flam, L., 'Fluvial Geomorphology of the Lower Indus Basin (Sindh, Pakistan) and the Indus Civilisation', in *Himalayas to the Sea: Geology, Geomorphology and the Quaternary*, ed. J. F. Shroder (New York, 1993), pp. 265–87

Frenez, Dennys, Gregg M. Jamison, Randall W. Law, Massimo Vidale and Richard H. Meadow, eds, *Walking with the Unicorn: Social Organization and Material Culture in Ancient South Asia* [Jonathan Mark Kenoyer Felicitation Volume] (Oxford, 2018)

Guha, Sudeshna, *The Marshall Albums: Photography and Archaeology* (Ahmedabad, 2010)

Gupta, S. P., *The Indus-Saraswati Civilization: Origins, Problems and Issues* (New Delhi, 1996)

Heyerdahl, Thor, *The Tigris Expedition: In Search of Our Beginnings* (London, 1980)

Jansen, Michael, Máire Mulloy and Günter Urban, eds, *Forgotten Cities on the Indus: Early Civilization in Pakistan from the 8th to the 2nd Millennium BC* (Mainz, 1991)

Jha, N., and N. S. Rajaram, *The Deciphered Indus Script: Methodology, Readings, Interpretations* (New Delhi, 2000)

Joshi, Jagat Pati, and Asko Parpola, eds, *Corpus of Indus Seals and Inscriptions*, vol. I: *Collections in India* (Helsinki, 1987)

Kennedy, Kenneth A. R., 'Skulls, Aryans and Flowing Drains: The Interface of Archaeology and Skeletal Biology in the Study of the Harappan Civilization', in Jonathan Mark Kenoyer, *Ancient Cities of the Indus Valley Civilization* (Karachi, 1998)

——, 'Uncovering the Keys to the Lost Indus Cities', *Scientific American* (July 2003), pp. 66–75

Kenoyer, Jonathan Mark, *Ancient Cities of the Indus Valley Civilization* (Karachi, 1998)

Khan, F., J. R. Knox, K. D. Thomas and J. C. Morris, *Sheri Khan Tarakai and Early Village Life in the Borderlands of North-west Pakistan*, ed. C. A. Petrie (Oxford, 2010)

Kinnier Wilson, J. V., 'Fish Rations and the Indus Script: Some New Arguments in the Case for Accountancy', *South Asian Studies*, III (1987), pp. 41–6

Kovach, Robert L., Kelly Grijalva and Amos Nur, 'Earthquakes and Civilizations of the Indus Valley: A Challenge for Archaeoseismology', in *Ancient Earthquakes*, ed. Manuel Sintubin, Iain S. Stewart, Tina M. Nierni and Erhan Altunel, Geological Society of America Special Paper 471 (Boulder, CO, 2010), pp. 119–27

Lahiri, Nayanjot, *Finding Forgotten Cities: How the Indus Civilization was Discovered* (Oxford, 2006)

——, ed., *The Decline and Fall of the Indus Civilization* (New Delhi, 2000)

McIntosh, Jane R., *A Peaceful Realm: The Rise and Fall of the Indus Civilization* (Boulder, CO, 2002)

——, *The Ancient Indus Valley: New Perspectives* (Santa Barbara, CA, 2008)

Mackay, E.J.H., *Further Excavations at Mohenjo-daro*, 2 vols (New Delhi, 1938)

Mahadevan, Iravatham, 'What do we Know about the Indus Script? *Neti Neti* ("Not This Nor That")', *Journal of the Institute of Asian Studies*, VII (1989), pp. 1–37
——, 'An Encyclopedia of the Indus Script', *The Book Review* [New Delhi], XIX (June 1995), pp. 9–12
——, 'Murukan in the Indus Script', *Journal of the Institute of Asian Studies*, XVI (1999), pp. 3–39
——, 'One Sees what one Wants To', *Frontline*, 11–24 November 2000, p. 125
Majeed, Tehnyat, ed., *Rediscovering Harappa: Through the Five Elements* (Lahore, 2016)
Marshall, John, 'First Light on a Long-forgotten Civilisation: New Discoveries of an Unknown Prehistoric Past in India', *Illustrated London News*, 20 September 1924, pp. 528–32, 548
——, *Annual Report of the Archaeological Survey of India, 1925–26: Exploration, Western Circle, Mohenjo-daro* (Calcutta, 1926)
——, *Mohenjo-daro and the Indus Civilization*, 3 vols (London, 1931)
Masson, Charles, *Narrative of Various Journeys in Balochistan, Afghanistan, and the Panjab*, vol. I (London, 1842)
Meadow, Richard H., 'The Domestication and Exploitation of Plants and Animals in the Greater Indus Valley, 7th–2nd Millennium BC', in *Forgotten Cities on the Indus: Early Civilization in Pakistan from the 8th to the 2nd Millennium BC*, ed. Michael Jansen, Máire Mulloy and Günter Urban (Mainz, 1991)
Miller, Naomi, 'The Use of Dung as Fuel: An Ethnographic Example and an Archaeological Application', *Paléorient*, X (1984), pp. 71–9
Mughal, Mohammed Rafique, *Ancient Cholistan: Archaeology and Architecture* (Lahore, 1997)
Nehru, Jawaharlal, *The Discovery of India* (London, 1946)
Parpola, Asko, *Deciphering the Indus Script* (Cambridge, 1994)
——, 'Indus Civilisation', in *Brill's Encyclopaedia of Hinduism*, ed. Knut A. Jacobsen, vol. IV (Leiden, 2012)
——, *The Roots of Hinduism: The Early Aryans and the Indus Civilization* (New York, 2015)
Parpola, Asko, B. M. Pande and Petteri Koskikallio, eds, *Corpus of Indus Seals and Inscriptions*, vol. III, parts 1 and 2: *New Material, Untraced Objects, and Collections Outside India and Pakistan* (Helsinki, 2010 and 2019)
Petrie, Flinders, 'Mohenjo-daro', *Ancient Egypt and the Near East* (1932), Part Two, pp. 33–40
Piggott, Stuart, *Prehistoric India to 1000 BC* (London, 1950)
Possehl, Gregory L., *Indus Age: The Writing System* (Philadelphia, PA, 1996)
——, *The Indus Civilization: A Contemporary Perspective* (New Delhi, 2003)
——, ed., *Harappan Civilization: A Contemporary Perspective* (New Delhi, 1982)
Rao, S. R., *The Decipherment of the Indus Script* (Bombay, 1982)
Ratnagar, Shereen, *Trading Encounters: From the Euphrates to the Indus in the Bronze Age* (New Delhi, 2004)
——, *The Magic in the Image: Women in Clay at Mohenjo-daro and Harappa* (New Delhi, 2018)

Ray, Satyajit, *The Unicorn Expedition, and Other Fantastic Tales of India* (New York, 1987)

Reade, Julian, ed., *The Indian Ocean in Antiquity* (London, 1996)

Renou, Louis, *Religions of Ancient India* (London, 1953)

Robinson, Andrew, *The Story of Writing: Alphabets, Hieroglyphs and Pictograms*, revd edn (London, 2007)

——, *Lost Languages: The Enigma of the World's Undeciphered Scripts*, revd edn (London, 2009)

——, *India: A Short History* (London, 2014)

——, 'Cracking the Indus Script', *Nature*, 526 (2015), pp. 499–501

——, 'Forgotten Utopia', *New Scientist*, 17 September 2016, pp. 30–33

Shah, Sayid Ghulam Mustafa, and Asko Parpola, eds, *Corpus of Indus Seals and Inscriptions*, vol. II: *Collections in Pakistan* (Helsinki, 1991)

Simpson, Edward, *The Political Biography of an Earthquake: Aftermath and Amnesia in Gujarat, India* (London, 2013)

Thapar, Romila, *Early India: From the Origins to AD 1300* (London, 2002)

Trautmann, Thomas R., *India: Brief History of a Civilization* (New York, 2011)

——, ed., *The Aryan Debate* (New Delhi, 2005)

Wells, Bryan K., *Epigraphic Approaches to Indus Writing* (Oxford, 2011)

Wheeler, Mortimer, *Still Digging: Interleaves from an Antiquary's Notebook* (London, 1955)

——, *The Indus Civilization*, 3rd edn (Cambridge, 1968)

Witzel, Michael, and Steve Farmer, 'Horseplay in Harappa: The Indus Valley Decipherment Hoax', *Frontline*, 30 September–13 October 2000, pp. 4–14

Woolley, Leonard, *Ur 'of the Chaldees'*, ed. P.R.S. Moorey (London, 1982)

Wright, Rita P., *The Ancient Indus: Urbanism, Economy, and Society* (New York, 2010)

Yadav, Nisha, 'Sensitivity of Indus Script to Site and Type of Object', *Scripta*, V (2013), pp. 67–103

The best website about the Indus civilization is www.harappa.com

▮▮▮ ACKNOWLEDGEMENTS

The author thanks Ben Hayes of Reaktion Books for suggesting the idea of this book and Aimee Selby for her excellent copy-editing.

PHOTO ACKNOWLEDGEMENTS

and Soban, the copyright holder of the image on p. 139, have published these online under conditions imposed by a Creative Commons Attribution-Share Alike 3.0 Unported license; Wikipedia Loves Art at the Brooklyn Museum, the copyright holder of the image on p. 80, has published it online under conditions imposed by a Creative Commons Attribution 2.0 Generic license.

Readers are free:

- to share – to copy, distribute and transmit these images alone

- to remix – to adapt these images alone

Under the following conditions:

- attribution – readers must attribute any image in the manner specified by the author or licensor (but not in any way that suggests that these parties endorse them or their use of the work).